Yves Klein

T0345506

Titles in the series Critical Lives present the work of leading cultural figures of the modern period. Each book explores the life of the artist, writer, philosopher or architect in question and relates it to their major works.

In the same series

Yves Klein

Nuit Banai

REAKTION BOOKS

For Nili Banai

Published by Reaktion Books Ltd
33 Great Sutton Street
London EC1V 0DX, UK
www.reaktionbooks.co.uk

First published 2014
Copyright © Nuit Banai 2014

Printed and bound in Great Britain by Bell & Bain, Glasgow

A catalogue record for this book is available from the British Library
ISBN 978 1 78023 293 5

Contents

Introduction: Klein the Paradox

My paintings represent poetic events or rather immobile witnesses,
silent and static witnesses of the very essence of movement and of free life,
which is the flame of poetry during the pictorial moment! My paintings
are the 'ashes' of my art.[1]

A painter must paint a single masterpiece, constantly: himself, and thus
become a sort of atomic battery, a sort of constantly radiating generator
that impregnates the atmosphere with his pictorial presence fixed in space
after its passage.[2]

In May 1962, in a slightly a perverse and somewhat Dadaesque
sequence of events, the Catalan artist Joan Miró confused Yves Klein
with the American Abstract Expressionist Franz Kline and sent his
young bride, Rotraut, a letter of condolence on the occasion of his
'death'. Kline passed away in New York City on 13 May, leaving Klein
the tragicomic task of responding to Miró's missive on 2 June with the
reassurance that he was still 'really alive'.[3] Only four days later, at the
age of 34, the French *enfant terrible* unexpectedly died of a heart attack
at his apartment on the rue Campagne-Première in Paris, leaving
many wondering if this was not his most mordant performance yet.

Considering the many provocations that propelled his
spectacular career, it would not have been implausible to imagine
that Klein, the only son of the painters Marie Joséphine Raymond
and Friedrich Franz Albert Klein, staged his own death. For one, he

had claimed to have 'invented' the monochrome, which had emerged more than 40 years earlier in the context of the Russian avant-garde and was independently resurrected after the Second World War by artists such as Claude Bellegarde and Ellsworth Kelly in France, Robert Rauschenberg and Ad Reinhardt in the United States, and Lucio Fontana and Piero Manzoni in Italy. Then there was the infamous *Epoca Blu* exhibition at the Galleria Apollinaire in Milan in 1957, at which Klein displayed eleven identical blue monochromes that he allegedly sold at different prices. The following year Klein scandalized the public by presenting an empty, whitewashed room devoid of traditional art objects, which he baptized *The Void*, at the Galerie Iris Clert in Paris. His notoriety as a hoaxster was sealed with *Leap into the Void* of 1960, the staged, photographic composite of the immaculately tailored artist suspended in a gravity-defying vault. Further aggravating public tastes, in 1960 Klein presented a performance known as the *Anthropometries* at one of Paris's ritziest venues, the Galerie Internationale d'Art Contemporain. Dressed in a dinner suit and accompanied by musicians performing his one-note 'monotone symphony', the artist gave precise instructions to nude female models covered in his signature blue paint who writhed sensually on the floor and left abstract painterly marks in their stead. With such a 'colourful' history, one might have easily suspected that Klein's sudden demise was just another flagrant abuse of the norms of bourgeois propriety for the sake of publicity.

The incredulity that accompanied Klein's passing is symptomatic of his life. Going hand in hand, his brash posturing and resolute exaltation of 'exasperating and utterly conscious artificiality' shaped his contemporaneous reception and continued to affect his posthumous assessment.[4] For some, Klein's variable identity was a stroke of brilliance and solid proof of his avant-garde credentials, but for many his apparent falsity and inability to maintain a stable persona cast a pall over his entire practice. His most intimate coterie accepted the fictive fabrication of his life as an integral part of his disposition. His close friend, Arman, recognized that 'Yves . . . was a total "mythomane". He could imagine having done things, even if he hadn't done them . . . If he'd dreamed them, he had done them.'[5] His long-term companion and collaborator, Bernadette Allain, put it this way: 'He had an amazing ability to live the imaginary. Perhaps in a very infantile way, but he really lived it.'[6] Meanwhile, artists of his generation in both Europe and the United States, among them Piero Manzoni, Jean Tinguely, Günther Uecker and Larry Rivers, embraced what they perceived as Klein's transgressive malleability and savvy understanding of the formidable role of marketing, branding and image management in the increasingly entwined mass cultural and aesthetic spheres. On the other side of the polemical fence, North American critics Jack Kroll and John Canaday and European critics such as Claude Rivière balked at the seeming irreconcilability of Klein's personal and conceptual melange. Searching for an unequivocal position that would resolve rather than entertain paradoxes, they found it difficult to make sense of the multiple strategies Klein kept constantly in play. These include, but are not reducible to, his insincere and often hyperbolic 'shenanigans' and earnest demonstrations of religious faith; embrace of trans-cendental philosophies like Zen and Rosicrucian cosmogony and a materialist bourgeois lifestyle; obstinate claims for originality and insouciant plagiarism of the writings of a motley group of figures such as Eugène Delacroix, Max Heindel and Gaston Bachelard; absorption of modernism's critical paradigms as his own opus, most notably the monochrome; and unrepentant enjoyment of mass-produced, petit-bourgeois pandering kitsch. Questions abounded: how could Klein attempt to copyright a readily available blue pigment (International Klein Blue), which had already permeated the aesthetic universes of Giotto and Stéphane Mallarmé, and at the same time urge artists to forego their individual egos and collaborate with one another? How could he rightfully sell 'immaterial zones of pictorial sensibility' for a kilogram of gold? And how could he become a knight in the conservative Order of St Sebastian and claim to be an avant-garde artist? To make sense of Klein's short but prodigious output, the paradoxical elements that constituted his art and life have, for the most part, been parsed, compressed and diverted into specific terrains of study as if keeping them isolated would somehow provide clarity.

During Klein's lifetime, his chief supporter, the art critic Pierre Restany, designated him the most important figure among the Nouveaux Réalistes (New Realists), a short-lived 'neo-Dada' movement founded by Restany and nine emerging artists on 27 October 1960 in Klein's apartment. To make his case for Nouveau Réalisme's mission of engendering 'new perceptual approaches to the real', Restany stressed the spiritual and mystical dimensions of Klein's work, to which he allocated utopian possibilities within France's post-war economic boom. Their symbiotic relationship helped launch both artist and critic and it is as hard to imagine Klein's ascent to international renown without the prose of Restany as it is to imagine Restany's emergence as the voice of his generation without Klein's work.[7] In recent years the grey zones of their alliance have been examined in order to clarify who influenced whom and when, but the fact remains that their ideas – however different – were mutually constitutive and helped both of them to refine their philosophies and advance their careers in those formative years.[8] While Restany's support eventually extended to other artists and architects in Europe and the United States, Klein was his first unequivocal *parti pris*. It is important to be clear, however, that Klein was not Restany's 'creation', a malleable minion who could dutifully embody and broadcast the critic's idea. On the contrary, Restany would not have been able to build such a long-lasting discursive edifice around Klein's practice if the artist had not taken part in the enterprise and provided the primary images and concepts.

In 1959, at the age of 31, Klein commenced one of his most well-known texts, 'Overcoming the Problematics of Art', with these pronouncements:

> It is inadequate to write or to say, 'I have overcome the problematics of art.' It is necessary to have done so. I have done so. Painting is no longer a function of the eye; it is the function of the one thing we may not possess within ourselves: our LIFE.[9]

For Restany, Klein's avant-garde claims for eliminating the gap between art and life were subsumed into a loosely argued theory for Nouveau Réalisme's status as the post-war resurgence of Dada and the centrality of the readymade as 'the basic element for a new expressive repertory'.[10] With critical hindsight, we can also approach the artist's statements from another perspective: his deliberately crafted connectivity with non-artistic practice and prodigious output of writings did more than situate him as an avant-garde artist fixated on dismantling the autonomy of art by subsuming it into the complexity of life. It also effectively transformed his own life into the very bedrock of his aesthetic persona.

This situation leads to all kinds of interpretive problems, most significantly whether to consider Klein's writings as irrefutable empirical data, absurd fabrications or aesthetic manifestations. At his death he left behind a cache of intimate journals, photo albums, personal and professional correspondence, press releases to his exhibitions, diagrams and sketches, films and a collection of essays that continue to reach out beyond the grave. If his paintings – along with all the other art objects, performances and statements – are but the 'ashes' of his art and have no independent meaning, what elements from the historical realm do we call upon to analyse them? And, in the context of this book, what do we make of Klein's fastidiously fashioned and retrospectively revised biographical trajectory? How do we decide whether to give more hermeneutical weight to Klein's elaborate discursive output or to the wider sphere of reception? This tension between 'the myth' and 'the man' may be a methodological conundrum that accompanies most interpretive endeavours, but it is a particularly thorny issue in Klein's case because he purposefully manipulated the relation between his art practice and his life and because he started to make art objects relatively late in his brief life. His entire oeuvre was produced between 1954 and 1962, or from the age of 26 to 34. Yet, as his autobiography would have it, most of the key concepts that endowed these works with meaning emerged earlier, in the course of Klein's formative years, while he was steeped in Catholicism, Rosicrucianism and Zen Buddhism. By and large, because of the brevity of his career, the prevailing understanding of Klein is based on painstaking attempts to analyse the ways in which the artist's self-professed adherence to an array of religious beliefs and philosophical systems shaped his art work and the constellation of discourses around it.

Like Restany, who dominated the Klein scholarship from the mid-1950s to his death in 2003, many others have also taken the artist's claim to spiritual illumination and transcendence as undisputed vantage points from which to understand his work. Throughout the years Klein has been formulaically described as a mystic, a seer or a visionary, one either fully ahead of his time or somehow existing in a privileged space of clairvoyance in its midst.[11] In recent years, however, some scholars have tried to extricate Klein's artwork from his writings and to analyse them as two equally constructed conceptual projects, while others have attempted to expand Klein's self-defined aesthetic universe by connecting his artwork more closely with other practitioners, intellectual frameworks and historical contexts of his time.[12] There has also been a concerted effort to recognize the relation between Klein's hybrid artistic production and almost every aesthetic movement that emerged in the 1950s and '60s, including performance art, happenings, body art, earth art, minimalism, conceptual art and installation.[13] In this sense Klein's position as a pivotal figure in the post-war period inserts him into the long-standing debate about the relationship between the historical avant-garde and the neo-avant-garde. Launched by the German literary critic Peter Bürger in the mid-1970s, the question of how to position the re-emergence of avant-garde strategies and visual paradigms (that is, readymade, collage, assemblage and mono-chrome) in the post-war context remains a dominant one in the field. For Bürger neo-avant-garde artists of the 1950s and '60s, such as Klein and Andy Warhol, were ineffective because they gave up the critical project of negating art's autonomous status in bourgeois society and integrating it into the praxis of life. Instead, according to Bürger, they became complicit with the institutional-ization of art and, worse, used the strategies and techniques of the historical avant-garde to do so. From this perspective the peak of modernism's revolutionary project is located in the actions of historical avant-garde artists such as Marcel Duchamp, Pablo Picasso, Aleksandr Rodchenko, René Magritte and John Heartfield, while everything following the Second World War degenerates toward an uncritical celebration of mass culture.[14] If Bürger's distressing diagnosis has been the subject of rigorous critique since its appearance, this critical biography continues to argue both for the relevance of post-war artistic production and Klein's vital role in creating new aesthetic concepts.[15] Rather than placing him as the penultimate step towards the complete deterioration of avant-garde art, I situate him first among a new generation. As part of this welcome sea change, Klein's precocious complexity has been recognized by an international group of artists, curators and scholars who have contributed to a more nuanced conception of his radicality through major exhibitions in Frankfurt, Los Angeles, London, Paris and Washington, DC. Following these new paths, it would not be too much of an exaggeration to argue that Klein transformed the field of art by simultaneously repudiating all the given terms that had sustained modernism throughout the early twentieth century and exploiting the porous channels between art and life in performative and paradoxical ways that contributed to the emergence of postmodernism and continue to serve as contemporary models. In this new role Klein becomes an avatar of the post-industrialist society that created the conditions of possibility for the present.

As important as it is to trace Klein's impact proactively and note his anticipation of the yet-to-come, there is no question that he firmly belonged to his historical moment. As this book suggests, in the context of the Long Sixties in France, Klein offered a singular approach to a set of artistic and historical questions that were shared by many artists of his generation well beyond the purview of Nouveau Réalisme. In his attempts to dismantle and de-materialize the unique and integral work of art and expand it into the order of publicity, display, performance, participation, architecture, the cinematic, linguistic and other discursive and contextual apparatuses, he was not only searching for a different definition of art, but another identity for the artist and his ever-elusive public. Perhaps one of his most crucial and understudied legacies, then, is the fabrication of his own identity as an aesthetic project. At various moments in his life, most often simultaneously, he inhabited the role of a bourgeois, *judoka*, painter, avant-garde artist, charlatan, collaborator, politician, poet, middle-class mystic, fascist and ultimate showman. Through complex circuits of meaning Klein synchronously associated himself with occult belief systems and a pragmatic market economy; the genealogy of a utopian avant-garde and the administrative, bureaucratized, spectacle-saturated realm of consumer culture. It is not so much that he crossed over between identities with no misgiving, sense of fraudulence or incongruity, but that he made visible the emergence of both a historical model of artistic identity and a public body based on paradox.

The contemporaneous writings of the French critic Roland Barthes provide an important theoretical armature that can help illuminate Klein's paradoxical inclinations, both in the ways he formulated his identities and his methods of broadcasting them to the public. If we remain attentive to Klein's manoeuvring, we note that he functioned very much like Barthes' definition of a photograph: a 'unique structure' that communicates a message by bringing together a 'source of emission, a channel of transmission, and a point of reception'.[16] Photography, in Barthes' view, is a medium in which the contested terms of structural autonomy and contingency are complementary and cooperative, existing side by side and informing one another. Within this framework it becomes evident that Klein communicated his identity as if he were a 'photographic message' – an image that gains its meaning from a literal reality but also operates in tandem with discursive codes and supports that are cultural and sociological. Following Barthes, it may be fruitful to consider that Klein's identity was linked to his particular biographical experiences, yet also trans-formed into a highly connotative image whose constellation of meanings was shaped by supplementary mechanisms.

What makes Klein's case so important is his ability to confound the existence of two messages – the literal and discursive – which Barthes terms 'the photographic paradox'. Based on Barthes' insights, we need to go beyond an understanding of Klein's identity as the simple complicity between a denoted message (a lived, 'natural' biography, or the literal) and a connoted message (a fictitious, 'cultural' artistic persona, or the discursive). Rather presciently from our perspective, Klein treats both the 'natural' and 'cultural' aspects of his identity like floating codes or random chains of signifieds that can be assembled, disassembled and re-assembled into assorted images. Even more radically, his identities were neither given nor unified but emerged only in the experience of their production. For these reasons Klein 'enunciated' his 'self' through various filters, catalysts, delivery systems and channels of mediation and was enormously concerned with the procedures through which he would be rendered visible and, hence, perceived and recognized as an artist. In this performative logic he not only crystallized the anomalies of the post-war period but paved the way for scores of contemporary artists, for whom artistic identity is not 'natural', 'essential' or 'conclusive' but is itself an aesthetic invention that is constituted in the act of utterance as a performative event. Though contemporaries Joseph Beuys and Andy Warhol contributed to a similar deconstruction of modernist art practices in West Germany and the United States by either mythologizing the link between life and art, on the one hand, or creating an ironic or deadpan distance between them, on the other, Klein's marshalling of a paradoxical and performative logic situates him as a critical case study.

The task of this book, then, is to foreground Klein's varied and variable aesthetic personas while providing an account of his life. The challenge, of course, is that Klein did not shed one persona and slip into the next in a neat and decisive chronological sequence, but manifested his hybrid identities at different intensities throughout his life. Certain aspects came to the fore and others receded at specific instances, yet it would be misguided to reduce Klein's logic of simultaneity to a strict temporal categorization or a unified sense of self. To contend with this unruly volatility, I have had to momentarily capture Klein in one static pose and foreground a particular identity in relation to the biographical context in which it was formulated and the principal art objects with which it was intertwined. It is my hope that this stop-motion technique will not hinder the reader from observing Klein as if through a kaleidoscope – to perceive a prismatic identity in which a tentative whole can only be constructed through a bricolage of unstable, luminous fragments.

1

Living on the Axis: Bourgeois and Bohemian, 1928–48

To discipline oneself

Is to take one-self for a disciple

And to take one-self for a disciple is to recognize

that we are two . . .[1]

Reflecting on his childhood in a questionnaire for the French magazine *Arts* in 1958, Yves Klein remarked that he was 'born into a milieu of painters and developed a taste for painting with a baby bottle'.[2] This rather clichéd foundational mythology is not uncommon in the annals of artistic biographies, but in Klein's case it was actually true. Although he adopted the moniker 'Yves: The Monochrome', the artist's upbringing was anything but monotonous or lacklustre. Born on the rue Verdi in Nice at his maternal grandparents' home on 28 April 1928, and raised in relative financial comfort and security, Yves Marie Klein's early years were shaped by a contradictory set of circumstances. Between 1928 and 1948 he not only grew up on the north–south geographic, political and cultural axis, but more profoundly in the push and pull between his parents' itinerant, bohemian lifestyles and the bourgeois home provided by his Aunt Rose.

His mother, Marie Joséphine Raymond (1908–1989), the youngest of two daughters, was born to Pierre Paul Raymond and Jeanne Emilie Raymond (née Giraud-Brun) in a small rural village called La Colle-sur-Loup in the département of Alpes-Maritimes.

With her older sister, Rose Raymond (1902–1993), she was raised in a middle-class neighbourhood in Nice in an apartment above a pharmacy owned by her father. Marie and Rose's grandfather had made his fortune selling flowers to the local perfume industry in the nearby town of Grasse. At the age of fifteen, through a serendipitous encounter with the artist Alexandre Stoppler in the Mediterranean coastal village of Cagnes-sur-Mer, Marie discovered her life's calling. Rose and her first husband, a local doctor with interests in Hinduism and yoga, were making a house call to tend to the ailing Stoppler and had brought Marie along. Like Auguste Renoir, Chaim Soutine and Amedeo Modigliani before her, Marie was seduced by the village's incandescent topography and, upon returning to Nice, acquired a box of paints. With her family's permission, she studied with Stoppard once a week and visited Cagnes on her own in the following summers. It was there that she met her future husband, Fred, at an outdoor party in 1925.

Friedrich Franz Albert Klein (1898–1990), known as 'Fred' or 'Frits', was born in Bandung, part of the Dutch East Indies, to Friedrich Franz Albert Klein, a German born in Hamburg who had Dutch nationality and had come to work on a plantation. There, he married a woman of Javanese descent named Emma Charlotte Klein (née Ploem). Fred's father died ten days before his birth and his mother married another Dutch cultivator, Jacob Roelof de Vries, who introduced him to the art of Vincent Van Gogh, Wassily Kandinsky and Paul Klee.[3] When he was only six, Fred and his sisters were sent to live in Holland and eventually the entire family relocated to Rotterdam in 1916 after the death of his stepfather, making it possible for Fred to pursue his artistic ambitions at the Royal Academy of Art in The Hague. In 1920 he moved to Paris and studied painting with André Lhote, an early adherent of Cubism, and in the Académie de la Grande Chaumière, a school founded by the Swiss painter Martha Stettler that attracted many expatriate artists. In 1924 he travelled to Cagnes and purchased La Goulette, a ruined building that he restored and transformed into his home and atelier.

On 26 October 1926, just over a year after their first meeting, Marie and Fred were married and moved to a studio in Montparnasse on the rue du Départ, in the same building as Piet Mondrian. Probably to spare doctor's costs, they returned to Nice for the birth of their only son and had Rose's husband officiate over the event. Yet the couple only spent a few months with their infant before deciding to return to Paris to advance Fred's blossoming career. A figurative painter with modest success, Fred had his first exhibition at the Galerie d'Art Français in Amsterdam in 1930, followed by a local debut that same year at the Galerie Minerve in Paris. The couple became acquainted with the French capital's bohemian circles, frequenting cafés like La Closerie des Lilas and La Coupole and socializing with Ecole de Paris artists such as Auguste Herbin and Jacques Villon. Marie later remembered dancing with her neighbour Piet Mondrian at Le Dôme, the renowned gathering spot for artists and intellectuals in Montparnasse.

The first two years of the young Yves' life were spent in Nice, in the care of his grandparents and his Aunt Rose, who lovingly nicknamed him 'Raton' ('Mouse') and to whom he would affectionately refer as 'Tantine' ('Aunty'). Rose Gasperini (née Raymond) was a devout Catholic who never had children of her own and was more financially solvent than her unconventional sister. Divorced by the time of Klein's birth, her maternal affection for her nephew was palpable and she was happy to become a doting second mother who could at once offer him stability and cater to his every caprice. Life in her care included nightly prayers, Mass on Sundays, devotion to the cult of St Rita (the patron saint of lost causes who had a strong following in the south of France) and induction into the rigid bourgeois principles that seemed woefully missing from his parents' milieu. 'It was she to whom [Klein] would return each time he had some need for the rest of his life, because with her he could find himself on solid ground again.'[4] Rose lavished Klein with gifts that his parents could not afford, leading to occasional conflicts with Marie, who accused her sister of 'trying to buy her son'.[5] Virtually every Klein biographer, including Thomas McEvilley, Sidra Stich and Annette Kahn, note that the presence of two distinct mother figures was both a bane and a blessing for the young lad. With Marie, Klein was allowed to roam freely in the wild landscape of Cagnes and follow his creative predilections, never having to obey a schedule or any kind of authority. Living with Rose in Nice, he was given strict parameters, a sense of religious piety and bourgeois respectability. Moving between their two homes and the peculiarities of their value systems, religious affiliations, outlook on child rearing and financial situations, he learned how to simultaneously be 'at home' (*Heimliche*) and 'un-homed' (*Unheimliche*) in both a bohemian and bourgeois environment. Living on this precarious axis during his formative years, he grasped the fine art of adapting to different expectations, assuming various identities and harnessing divergent sets of codes – with no sense of duplicity and with absolute charm – when it suited him most.

Klein's shuttling between distinct social situations continued incessantly throughout the next decade. In 1930 the toddler was brought to Paris when his parents relocated to a house built by Le Corbusier on boulevard Masséna. Still struggling financially, they moved to the suburb of Fontenay-aux-Roses in 1931 before uprooting once again and establishing themselves in the sunny climate of the Côte d'Azur between 1932 and 1936. During these years, while Marie studied at the National School for the Decorative Arts in Nice and enrolled in a correspondence course to become certified as an art teacher, Fred painted in his studio at La Goulette. Worried about her nephew's proper rearing under such irregular circumstances, Rose provided financial support for a religious education at a private school in Nice and brought him to see his parents in Cagnes on weekends. In 1937 the family once again migrated north, this time to the Paris suburb of Montrouge and a house full of artists' studios, including those of the Hungarian sculptor and architect Etienne Beöthy and the French abstract painter Jean Dewasne. Before the year was out, unable to pay rent, they sold their furniture and relocated to Cagnes. As might have been expected, Marie and Fred's hiatus from Paris did not last long and they were soon collaborating on a fresco for the Pavilion of the Alpes-Maritimes at the International Exhibition dedicated to Arts and Technology in Modern Life (25 May–25 November 1937).

Despite the devolving value of the franc, anxieties about Germany's escalating militarization and the Spanish Civil War raging just across the Pyrenees, Marie recalled that 'Yves had a very happy childhood in the old town of Cagnes where he felt absolutely free . . . [He] was the leader of the band, they called him "captain" with his cap and sword-belt . . .'.[6] Looking up to their 'leader', the children would ask '"Yves, what shall we do?" and [he] would give them orders, "Meet in front of the castle with bows and arrows."'[7] That summer was indeed a joyful one for the nine-year-old, who did not appear to be particularly gifted in either painting or drawing but began to emulate his parents' creativity in other ways. At a fair organized by Cagnes' artistic community, he organized a children's theatre, Le Théâtre des Gnomes (The Theatre of the Dwarfs), with his friends Michel Gaudet and Hervé Germain in a local cellar. Inspired by the adventures of cartoon characters Tintin, The Three Musketeers and Mandrake the Magician, Klein became the director of this troupe and animated the other village children by concocting extravagant scenarios for them to perform. Even as a child, friends recall that Klein had a magnetic personality and 'the power to convince people by his charm'. He was thus 'always surrounded by a group of children who looked to him for leadership', a role that he enjoyed thoroughly.[8] Unfortunately he did not have the same flair or commitment to his school work and his mediocre results troubled his Aunt Rose. There was very little she could do, however, as in 1938 his parents moved to a house at 116 rue d'Assas in Paris, adjacent to the Jardin du Luxembourg, and took their ten-year-old son with them. Klein's assimilation into his parents' carefree lifestyle was disastrous. With very little disciplining from Marie and Fred and his own indifference to the regiment of studying, Klein's scholastic achievements at the Alsation school in which he was enrolled continued to decline. His teachers noted that he was 'lazy' and 'intolerable' and let his parents know that it was 'inadmissible that Yves' notebook is never signed, that he arrives late and does not work'.[9] Eventually, with no improvement and a rebellious attitude to boot, he was expelled and had to complete the academic year elsewhere. Before too long, however, the family returned to Cagnes for their summer holidays and Klein was freed from the humdrum toils of school.

Paradoxically, France's declaration of war on Germany on 3 September 1939 ushered in a period of relative stability for Klein. Between 1939 and 1943 Marie and Fred decided to remain in the Côte d'Azur, now part of the Vichy government's free zone. Though goods and food became scarcer and the family had to sell La Goulette and rent an older house in the neighbouring village of Hautes-de-Cagnes, Klein returned to his old habits, living with his Aunt Rose and attending religious school in Nice on weekdays and spending weekends with his parents. Perhaps the trickiest question to answer is whether Klein's life was cut into two distinct parts that were never made into an integrated whole or if he was able to weave them into a fluid framework that he wore like a second skin. How, as a child, did he make sense of these contradictory milieus that would remain polarizing forces during his entire life?

Not only will we never know the answers to these questions but we also want to avoid a psychoanalytic reading of Klein that tries to pinpoint the ontological 'origins' for his life and art. Instead, with

Roland Barthes as our methodological guide, let us consider two photographs from roughly the same period and note how Klein constructed his identity by internalizing and animating the codes of spectacularization. According to Barthes, knowing that an image is about to be produced, a sitter fashions another 'version' of him or herself specifically for the camera. In the same way, Klein 'constitutes himself in the process of "posing" . . . instantaneously [making] another body for [himself]' when observed by a lens.[10] Case in point: in a studio portrait taken on the day of his First Communion (25 May 1939), he is a well-groomed, doe-eyed boy with a starched white shirt and a dark suit, his hair parted perfectly on the side, a rosary draped on his arm and an open Bible in his hands. We can speculate that Klein's image of docility and refine-ment helped him adapt smoothly to the pampered life offered to him in Nice, a town whose agreeable climate attracted a privileged class who enjoyed afternoon tea and strolls on the Promenade des Anglais (English Promenade). Yet this was a life in which he also felt suffocated and from which he longed to escape. Meanwhile a snapshot taken in the Cagnes landscape (circa 1938) shows an equally well-dressed youngster who, despite the perfectly matching white ensemble and his captain's cap, stands his ground with hands smugly in pockets and gazes obstinately at the camera. This is the ruffian who sporadically ran away from his parents' home, once taking off by bicycle to discover St-Dalmas-le-Selvage in the Alps, and would sometimes be gone for days. We may presume that Klein's independent attitude was more in keeping with the laissez-faire laxity and imaginative allure of his parents' world, a model that he tried to emulate but from which he felt repeatedly rejected. Most important, what we glean from these two striking images is Klein's intuitive grasp that contemporary identity is a type of active image production. Whether posing for an actual camera lens or internalizing the lens as the tacit mode of a mediatized existence, Klein's identity becomes a 'social game', one in which posing, knowing that one is posing and wanting the viewer to know that one is posing in no way disrupt a presumption of individuality.[11] As Barthes reminds us, 'in front of the lens, I am at the same time: the one I think I am, the one I want others to think I am, the one the photographer thinks I am, and the one he makes uses to exhibit off his art.'[12] Rather than suffering from 'inauthenticity' or feeling a kind of 'imposture', as Barthes laments in his own case, Klein embraced the productive paradoxes and performative possibilities that materialize from the 'social game' of such lenticular fragmentation.[13]

As many fled Paris for the south of France, Cagnes became an enclave for exiled artists of all nationalities, among them Hans Hartung, Heinrich Maria Davringhausen and his wife Laure, Arnold Clerx and his wife Jacoba van Velde, Kees Kelk, Jean Villeri and Simone, and Geer van Velde. The neighbouring village of Grasse welcomed Alberto Magnelli, Jean Arp and Sophie Taeuber-Arp, Sonia and Robert Delaunay, Max Ernst and Nicolas de Staël and his family. Klein's parents became especially close to Staël and his wife, Jeannine Guillou, a fellow 'Niçoise' whom Marie had known for many years. Her son, Antoine Tudal (né Antek Tesler), who was now one of Klein's playmates, was duly enlisted to join the revitalized *Théâtre des Gnomes*, a staple of the adolescents' wartime entertainment. With Antek, Klein picked up discarded canvases and, grasping the stretcher braces, transformed them into knights' shields. He also composed short poems, such as 'Silence', written when he was eleven years old.

Klein's life was barely disrupted during the Second World War, as his family did not suffer any grievous loss and thankfully remained intact. Though xenophobic tensions agitated their artistic community and led to the formation of 'local' and 'foreign' art associations in the region, the Kleins' only immediate hardship was the pervasive austerity. This was especially true when they returned to their rue d'Assas apartment in Paris in June 1943, where they lived through the end of the war with no heat and nourished themselves from food purchased on the black market or provisions sent from the countryside. When a stranger purchased three paintings for 4,500 francs, they were able to live on kidney beans and tomatoes through the summer of 1944.[14]

Klein rediscovered the capital with curiosity and relish and wrote long letters to his aunt entitled 'Connaissance de Paris' (Knowledge of Paris), which detailed his walks on both the Left and Right Banks.[15] Though there is scant primary evidence regarding Klein's experience of living under German occupation, the historical state of exception touched his life all the same. In 1944, Klein enrolled at the École du Génie Civil in Paris, a preparatory school that trains students to pass the baccalauréat exam and enter the Merchant Marine Academy. Klein's plans were derailed, however, when his parents sent him to Milhars in the Tars region during the tumultuous months of the Liberation of Paris (June–August), and he eventually failed the baccalauréat exam. Far from the capital, he heard stories about the Resistance and had to explain that his name was of Dutch and not Jewish origin.[16] Still in Tars between 19 and 24 August, when the Germans surrendered, he experienced the Liberation through the buoyant narratives of others. Not wanting to be left out, he apparently returned to Paris carrying a grenade hidden in a loaf of bread.[17] In the intense exuberance of post-war Paris, Klein dabbled in jazz piano and dancing in the clubs of Saint-Germain-des-Prés. In 1945, as Marie Raymond's artistic career began to flourish with her participation at the Salon des Surindépendants, the family's small third-floor apartment on the rue d'Assas became a lively site for weekly get-togethers. Klein rubbed elbows with the newly emerging group of non-figurative artists Hans Hartung, Jean Dewasne, Jean Deyrolle and Gérard Schneider, who had their first exhibition (*La Jeune Peinture Abstraite*) at the gallery of Denise René in 1946. From that moment, Marie Raymond's Monday-night salons, *les lundis de Marie Raymond*, turned into a staple of Parisian social life and, between 1946 and 1954, the Kleins hosted almost every foreign visitor who passed through town along with virtually every Parisian luminary. Though his father was an adept figurative painter and his mother established herself as a leading force in the coterie of abstraction, everyone was welcomed at their soirées and Klein might easily have mingled with an assortment of cultural practitioners of different generations and artistic inclinations, like Francis Picabia, Pierre Soulages, Charles Estienne, Serge Poliakoff, Eugène Ionesco, Denise René, Colette Allendy, Iris Clert, François Dufrêne, Raymond Hains and Jacques Villeglé.

Though this art world was at his fingertips, in the summer of 1946, at the age of eighteen, Klein was both jobless and directionless and there is little indication that he was contemplating a life in the arts. His life partitioned between the poles of bohemia and the bourgeoisie, he spent a leisurely summer in London with his parents, three months as an au pair in Sevenoaks, Kent, and then visited Amsterdam before returning to Nice to work at his aunt's new business: La Librarie Radio-Son. The re-married Rose, now known as Madame Tamarasco, continually worried about her nephew's solvency and created a special literature section in her husband's appliance store where she employed Klein as a sales-person. As one of his close friends from the period, Claude Pascal recalls, 'Klein did what he wanted. He ordered [books] more for himself than for the business.'[18] In the recollections of another close friend, Armand Pierre Fernandez, who in 1948 shortened his name to 'Armand' and, following a typographical error in an art catalogue of 1958, became known simply as 'Arman', Klein only worked for around two hours a day and few people ever stopped by the appliance store to purchase books.[19] He was thus able to read at his leisure, his tastes ranging from the poetry of Jacques Prévert to science fiction; but he was also following artistic developments, as suggested by the gift he offered Arman for his birthday in 1948: the catalogue *Le Surréalisme en 1947*, which accompanied the seminal exhibition at the Galérie Maeght and had Marcel Duchamp's famous foam rubber bosom (*Prière de Toucher*) on the cover.[20]

Indulged by his aunt, Klein manned the book department according to his whims, which left him free to pursue his two main interests: dancing to the jitterbug in local nightclubs and courting young women. In 1947 he decided to enrol in a judo programme offered by the Nice police athletic league, a choice that became a crucial turning point in his life: not only did he befriend Claude Pascal and Arman, two other judo aficionados who became his inseparable companions, but he discovered a new passion. Although the least naturally able of the three, Klein immersed himself in the recently imported Japanese martial art, which offered him an arena distinct from both his parents' artistic scene and his aunt's world of bourgeois norms. He attended classes three times a week, quickly becoming proficient and progressing from white belt (2 September 1947), to yellow belt (19 December 1947), to orange belt (4 May 1948), to green belt (24 September 1948). With a few pauses to hitchhike throughout Italy and complete a year of military service at Lake Constance in Germany, Klein continued practising judo and advanced to blue belt (22 October 1950), followed by brown belt (30 August 1951) and eventually black belt (16 June 1952).

This sustained engagement with judo inspired Klein, Arman and Pascal to steep themselves in mystical studies. Between 1947 and 1948, while attending three different judo clubs in Nice, they explored Zen and Zen Buddhism and read about Zen Buddhism's historical development in Japan, considered astrology and eventually discovered the book *La Cosmogonie des Rose-Croix* by Max Heindel (1865–1919). This hermetic tome became a spiritual guide for the triumvirate, who called themselves the 'Triangle Group' and found a mentor in Louis Cadeaux, a chemical engineer and adept of Rosicrucianism known locally by his nickname 'Rose-Croix'. Like many such initiations, the first meeting with Cadeaux took on extraordinary proportions, and its mystical tenor should be taken with a grain of salt. Supposedly, Klein tracked him down after hearing about the septuagenarian at his aunt's store, the three young men knocked on his door late at night after practising judo, and when the elder man responded with the question 'What can I do for you?' Klein purportedly declared, 'We want to understand', to which Cadeaux responded, 'Ah! Come in, my children!'[21] Once admitted, Cadeaux became their spiritual advisor and they continued to visit him twice a week for about a year. After introducing them to the basics of Rosicrucianism and teaching them the art of casting horoscopes and practising meditation, he decided that they were ripe for the next step and recommended that they contact the Rosicrucian Society of Oceanside, California. In June 1948 Klein and Pascal joined the society, while the more pragmatic Arman abandoned the venture. For three years the two studied daily, followed a rigorous correspondence course that entailed sending their worksheets to California for review, and were regularly mentored by Cadeaux. From 1951 until mid-1953, when Klein's membership lapsed, he continued to receive his monthly lessons but did not return them for review. More than a passing episode in his formation, Klein became a devoted disciple of the *Cosmogonie* and its esoteric beliefs and referred to this 'initiation' for the rest of his life.

Thomas McEvilley has done a prodigious job of relating Max Heindel's theories to Klein's art. He argues that between 1948 and 1958, when Klein 'discovered' his next mentor, the philosopher Gaston Bachelard, he was overwhelmingly shaped by his induction into Rosicrucianism and tried to deliberately translate this belief system into a form of artistic expression.[22] As he crafted the myth of his own identity, Klein 'would read this book for hours every day. He would read it for entire nights. You could see the light in his window from the street. At two or three in the morning he was still reading. He was deeply penetrated by Rosicrucianism.'[23] While this system may have indeed sustained Klein's spiritual and philosophical inclinations, and certainly played a role in his search for an artistic vocabulary, one should be wary of trying to explain his entire practice as a literal equation of Rosicrucianism. His allegiance to this occult system helped him craft one among many artistic personas, and his art may be, at one level, an articulation of Heindel's system; but it is also substantially independent of it and very often does not coincide with it. Again, drawing on the structural analysis offered by Roland Barthes, '*who speaks* (in the narrative) is not *who writes* (in real life) and *who writes* is not *who is*.'[24] To conflate Klein's life with his art, without considering the language of art as both a particular system of signification and a performative moment of locution, is to miss out on Klein's multiple 'realisms'.

Sometime between 1947 and 1948, a much recounted episode with Arman and Pascal reveals Klein's dexterous mastery of the two models that structured his early life. In a fertile process of self-discovery, he spent long hours on the roof of Arman's residence meditating in an attempt to reach a mindful state. He also tried to overcome his physical limits by spending long nights staring at the moon, fasting and abstaining from smoking, drinking and eating meat. Along with occasional hallucinations, Arman recalled that at times these exercises made the trio feel as if they were casting off their physical bodies, levitating, or entering the void.[25] When lying on the beach during one of these instances, the three fancifully divided the world among themselves according to Heindel's three categories: vegetable, animal and mineral. Pascal, the poet, became the proprietor of the vegetable world and the dominion of words; Arman appropriated both the animal realm and the earth; and Klein 'signed' the blue sky of Nice as part of his mineral empire.[26] This event may have been purely whimsical for the two other title holders, but for Klein it became a decisive act. He came to consider the Azur a limitless zone that could engender individual freedom and bestowed the colour blue with the ability to dematerialize all boundaries and create a sensation of pure presence. In this spirit, and not long after the discovery of the prehistoric caves at Lascaux in the Dordogne, the basement of Arman's father's furniture store, where the three young men frequently consorted, became a 'cave' and 'temple' whose ceiling Klein painted pale blue. With Pascal, he also decorated one wall with hand- and footprints, while Arman painted images of tools assembled in the shape of a tree on another. These symbols – along with the sun, moon, stars, punctuation marks, palm trees and baobabs – soon ornamented Klein and Pascal's shirts, which they paraded through Nice as a manifestation of their enlightened condition.

As peculiar as these activities may seem, Klein did not treat them lightly. The moment when he 'signed his name on the underside of the sky' was his 'greatest' and most 'beautiful art work'.[27] His sentiment of owning the sky, the very symbol of natural freedom, meant that he 'began to hate the birds' that shared the space and ruined its perfect stillness, and stipulated that '[They] must be eliminated.'[28] These comments may rightfully give us pause if we remark that Klein's obsession with the blue sky as a space of absolute liberty is expressed in the administrative terms of property rights and ownership. Yet we need only be reminded of his upbringing in the foyer of both art and commerce, or bohemia and the bourgeoisie, to understand these tensions. From an early age Klein inhabited a paradoxical persona in which freedom and dominance went hand in hand, a double dynamic linked to his rearing and the accelerating consumer culture of the post-war era.

If there is no evidence that Klein had any painterly output in this period (there are only a few poems and his Rosicrucian notebook decorated with a blue cardboard disc), he revised and dramatized his artistic evolution in his text 'Overcoming the Problematics of Art' (1959) by narrating these seminal years in the following way:

In 1946 I was painting or drawing either under the influence of my father, a figurative painter of horses in landscapes or of beach landscapes, or under the influence of my mother, an abstract painter of compositions of forms and color. At the same time, 'COLOR,' the sensuous pure space, winked an eye at me irregularly, yet with stubborn persistence. This sense of the complete freedom of pure space exerted upon me such a powerful attraction that I painted monochrome surfaces to see, with my own eyes to SEE what was visible in the absolute.[29]

What is fascinating about this statement is that Klein did not consider this rewriting of his own history a falsification. Because his art and his life were intermeshed as a creative act, he felt free to take artistic licence with his own biography, even if others (especially art historians) consider it a form of deception.[30] For one, his early years had taught him how to take advantage of paradoxical syntaxes in order to fabricate and legitimate his own aesthetic concepts and identities. But most important, Klein approached his own biography as a type of narrative through which he travelled as a 'persona', 'participant' or 'image', rather than a unified psychological essence. In that sense, the illusion of chronological time was completely unimportant; his desire was not to conform to the referential order of reality but to 'perform' within the open source of discourse.

2

In Search of 'Self': Becoming a *Judoka*/Artist, 1948–52

The enthusiast can only vibrate in this where there are neither
fundamentals nor principles. He does not reflect, does not calculate,
does not speak, and does not provide explanations; he acts.[1]

For the next four years of his life, between 1948 and 1952, Klein's
peregrinations were buoyed by his dedication to judo. Though
he had attained a green belt while living in Nice, he dreamed
of travelling by horseback to Japan and studying in the official
Kodokan Institute in Tokyo. In search of his calling and with his
Aunt Rose's steady financial support, he vagabonded across Europe
with occasional stopovers in Paris or Nice to visit his friends and
family. As the art historian Benjamin H. D. Buchloh rightfully
notes, 'Klein's aspiration to be perceived as a *judoka*/artist made
him the neo-avant-garde's first *japoniste*, one situated between the
ancient culture of judo as a ritualistic performance of war and the
contemporary condition of Hiroshima.'[2] Yet Klein did not contrive
the *judoka*/artist identity overnight but spent four years, filled
with recurring bouts of uncertainty and anxiety, before he assumed
the pose.

Between the ages of twenty and twenty-four, unable to commit
to a specific path or to inhabit a singular identity, Klein gathered
and appropriated assorted materials, concepts and attitudes: a
steadfast Catholicism mixed with an adherence to Rosicrucianism
and a growing, if still rather tentative, interest in Zen Buddhism.

These spiritual rudiments from Western and Eastern traditions were intermeshed with Klein's interest in colour, an immersion in Paris's burgeoning artistic scene and an uncanny ability to turn anything and everything into an aspect of his artistic persona. It would be fair to say that between 1948 and 1952 Klein was neither an artist nor a *judoka* but a consumer and collector of citations and codes. Yet, in these fretful and fateful years, he decisively grasped that the 'self' is both an image and a social space fabricated from a constellation of practices and narratives. In fabricating the persona of *judoka*/artist, Klein sought ways to create images and construct spaces that could entertain both anachronistic and contemporary modes of seeing and knowing.

Short of means to accomplish the costly journey to Japan, Klein set off on an almost year-long detour in England and Ireland. Rather tangentially, this came about because he wanted to easily communicate with the Japanese intelligentsia when he arrived in Tokyo and had learned that they spoke English. Since Arman had by now enrolled at the Ecole du Louvre in Paris, Klein set off to London in November 1949, accompanied by his compatriot Claude Pascal. The duo lodged in a boarding house in Earl's Court and, with the help of his well-connected parents, Klein secured an apprenticeship with the frame-maker Robert Savage. Despite his reticence to adopt his parents' métier and his rather elementary responsibilities chez Savage, Klein received a technical crash course in constructing and polishing wooden frames, mixing pigments, employing fixatives and varnishes and working with gilding and gold leaf. If we are to believe his letters to Aunt Rose, Klein's days during his five months in London were uncharacteristically well-organized and replete with activities. He worked at Savage's store from Monday to Saturday from 9am until 6pm with an hour-long break for lunch at 1pm, took English classes on Monday and Wednesday evenings from 6:30 to 9:30pm, and practised judo every Tuesday and Friday evening from 7pm until 10pm as well as every Sunday morning.[3] This gruelling schedule, and the fact that he had barely enough to eat, did not hinder him from completing his coursework for the Rosicrucian Society, ameliorating his English at the Centre Franco-Anglais and visiting art institutions such as the National Gallery, British Museum, Victoria & Albert Museum and the Tate Gallery.[4]

In later years Klein would attribute great meaning to this period of artistic training. 'It was during this year at the "SAVAGE" studio that I perceived the illumination of matter as a profoundly physical quality.'[5] Though there is no extant evidence to prove this, Klein would subsequently maintain that after a day of work with Savage,

> I returned home to my room in the evenings, I did monochrome pastels on pieces of white cardboard and also increasingly used a lot of pastels . . . It seemed to me that, in pastel, each grain of pigment remained free and individual without being killed by the fixative medium.[6]

Claude Pascal also recalls that Klein made his first monochromes while working for Savage and considered their display in the boarding house his first exhibition. The mythical story goes that Klein went into their bathroom one evening and, after a long time, returned carrying small pieces of square paper, each covered with a single hue of gouache paint (blue, orange and green), and exclaimed, 'I have found it.'[7] James Shorrocks, another of Klein's London pals, remembers this event too. 'He just took a piece of cardboard and painted over it with blue . . . and then pinned it onto the wall with drawing pins and said, "I like that. I'm sure there's something there."'[8] Like many of Klein's later artistic forays, there appeared to be some confusion about whether he meant these as a joke.[9]

Such explorations did not distract him from his ultimate goal and, in mid-April 1950, he and Pascal hitchhiked to Ireland with the manifest objective of learning to ride horses. As far-fetched as it sounds, Klein's and Pascal's ambition was to become expert equestrians, purchase stallions in Morocco and follow the Silk Route on horseback all the way to Japan. Finally crossing the Irish Sea after a stopover in Liverpool, they struck a deal to clean stables and pick potatoes in exchange for riding lessons at a horse farm called 'Jockey-Hall', in County Kildare, the heart of Ireland's horse breeding and training region. With few distractions, Klein improved his English by memorizing ten words a day and making diligent efforts to write his diary in the foreign language. The promised riding lessons were few and far between, however, and even their continued judo practice could not mask their growing frustrations at their negligible progress and the frequent rain.

It appears that Klein and Pascal had a falling out and, as the months progressed, could not abide each other's company. The crisis most probably unfolded over their difference in temperament, as Pascal's apathy and general fatigue did not sit well with the heartier Klein. To make sense of the growing rift, Klein drew upon his religious faith, which seems to have given him direction and succour. Quoting the Gospel of St Luke, he noted that 'From all of this, I reach the following conclusion: I do not want to take care of other people's affairs and "see a mote in another's eye" because if the continuation of this proverb is true, what a monstrous fellow I must be!!'[10] The long hours of solitude contributed to a period of intense introspection during which the tenets of Christianity were very much a staple of Klein's thinking.

> Defying Evil needs to be my motto. I can no longer imagine being capable of hating anything, but too many tiny interior voices continue to murmur. If only my jaw could remind me, with each mouthful swallowed, that I eat the body of Christ! I am not ripe at all. Too young! . . . Faith! Faith! If only we could conserve and expand it every day.

(Klein's ten words for Friday, 11 August, included 'motto = *devise*, to challenge = *défier*, evil = *mal*, to hum = *murmurer*, jaw = *mâchoire*, mouthful = *bouchée*, ripe = *mûr*.)[11]

Throughout this difficult time, Klein reflected on the relation between anger and tranquillity and the way antagonism towards others leads to a negative rapport with oneself. His induction into Rosicrucianism and Catholicism did not seem to impede his embrace of other models of thought. As his diaristic ruminations reveal, the 22-year-old was learning how to make sense of his contradictory emotions.

> When the spirit of discord arises, it's a strange sentiment; it's a fact that it appears as suddenly and sharply as a bolt of lightning. I don't know its origin or what provokes it, I only know that it's extremely difficult to undo it. When I feel it coming, I desensitize myself; I chase all emotions away in order to analyse the events and reasons that have produced this state.[12]

These statements reveal Klein's restless search for a persona that could straddle dissonance and composure and for whom judo and abstract painting would soon represent such contradictory forms of self-presentation.

Though he accused Pascal of being trapped in his 'own spirit of discord', Klein's diary from the period reveals his own melancholia and wavering self-confidence. 'More and more', he writes,

> I am aware that I have nothing, neither a gift for anything, nor a facility for anything . . . It is frightful . . . it causes anxiety. I have only one thing to do, cosmogony and the constant study of the marvelous science that I have at my disposal! To draw, to play music, is too free a course for my imagination which lacks practical applications.[13]

Klein's doubt about his aesthetic inclinations was compounded by his realization that to be a skilled painter required a good deal of effort. It is unclear where he may have found materials in the Irish countryside, but his diary suggests that he pursued painting with some irritability.

> This afternoon and this morning I painted, only painted, and thought hard about this! The result is very depressing because it is very difficult to paint, more difficult than anyone can imagine . . . In painting you give your energy, and, in addition, something else. I don't know exactly what takes all your force from you.[14]

A letter to his friend Arman suggests that Klein did not consider these experiments with painting a serious endeavour and that he was not really contemplating a life in the arts. 'You are lucky', he confided, 'because you know what you want. You want to be a painter. For me it's more difficult because with judo and spirituality it is a longer journey. I do not know if I will succeed.'[15]

Klein left Ireland quite abruptly at the end of August 1950, possibly after another row with Pascal, who joined him in London a month later. Under constant financial duress, alleviated slightly by food packages sent by Aunt Rose, Klein resumed work at Savage's store and continued his study of English until the end of the year. Preceding his return to France in December, he sent Arman a home-made monochrome postcard with the message, 'The year 1951 will be a pink massacre.' The year did not start out so brightly, however, as Pascal contracted tuberculosis and had to be confined to a sanatorium, delaying their trip to Japan indefinitely. Klein would probably have ventured there alone if he had had the funds, but his only source of income was his aunt's generosity. He was not too shy to take advantage of it, but it also meant that he had to account for his perennial lack of direction. 'I have not yet decided anything about my future situation, and I assure you this is very difficult', he wrote to Tantine. 'Please send some money, 5,000 old francs, for example.'[16]

With fresh resources, Klein travelled to Spain on 3 February 1951, and after taking in the sights – the Prado, Escorial, Toledo – he returned to Madrid with the intention of studying Spanish and rented a room at 6 calle de Puebla. At first he was enchanted by his situation: 'I have a charming room on the third floor. Below is a very affordable restaurant. The entire building seems to be filled with students. In one word, everything is really delightful.' Within a month, however, his sentiments turned sour and he was calling his room 'Siberia'. He divulged his discouragement to his diary:

> I don't feel like doing anything today and I'm not able to make myself study. The days pass and I am still without work! I came here for nothing . . . I've reached a firm decision. If in less than eight days I haven't found anything, I will leave to discover America.[17]

Following this outlandish ultimatum, Klein's luck changed and he began giving private French lessons to a few students. Even better, he was offered his first salaried position as a judo instructor at the Bushido Kwai, a school for judo and jiu-jitsu. As time passed he became friendly with the owner of the club, Fernando Franco de Sarabia, whose father was a publisher. He also kept company with a certain Joaquim, a Spanish student his age identified only by his first name, and together they went to bull fights, museums, cinemas, bars and the great literary and intellectual hub of Madrid – El Café Gijón.

It was during this Spanish sojourn that Klein may have come up with the idea of making monochrome paintings that would be exhibited to 'appropriate music'.[18] Was this a reference to the yet-unwritten and unperformed one-note 'Monotone Symphony' that Pierre Henry would compose for Klein in 1957? Intrigued by his declarations and convinced that he was in the presence of a recognized artist, Joaquim insisted on seeing Klein's work. Never one to shun attention, Klein claims to have shown Joaquim a few monochromes painted on cardboard. This personal 'exhibition' did not go over too well and Klein quickly made a small landscape watercolour of Toledo as a peace offering. Despite this failed effort at convincing others of his singular concept, Klein's fixation with colour was blooming and he was starting to make lateral connections between colour, language and emotional intensity. For example, a fairly amateur attempt at Symbolist poetry titled 'Espagne' (Spain) associates colour with a range of feelings, including anger, jealousy and tranquility.

One day the blue sky fell to earth
And from its wound blood gushed forth.
It was dazzling and sparkling red.
There was also some black there where it coagulated.
A pool of blood. It was Spain.
When they looked at each other it was violet flashes.
The music was jealous.
And in the peace of the blue reigned the anger of the red.[19]

The poem's simple narrative foregrounds the power of colour to materialize sensations. Drawing upon somewhat conventional associations, with red signifying pain and anger and blue a peaceful existence, Klein was setting the stage for the more elaborate meditation of 'My Position Between Line and Color' (1958). In this subsequent text, which followed on the heels of his intense blue period, Klein approached colour as a direct and unmediated sensation. He notes that lines are the 'psychological boundaries, our historic past, our education, our skeletal framework; they are

our weaknesses and our desires, our faculties and our contrivances'.
In contrast,

> color . . . bathes in a cosmic sensibility . . . [It] is sensibility
> become matter – matter in its first primal state . . . Colors
> alone inhabit space, whereas the line only travels through it
> and furrows it. The line travels through infinity, whereas color
> is infinity. Through color I experience total identification with
> space; I am truly free.[20]

The seeds for Klein's preoccupation with the infinite may have
been sown by the anachronistic system of Rosicrucianism, which
he continued to study during his four months in Spain. But Klein
was not without an eye on the contemporary world and everything
he observed became fodder for his creative purposes. An American
demonstration of supersonic planes flying over Madrid led him
to surmise that 'Soon time (which can really be called the fourth
dimension) will be conquered, and then we will no longer have
past or future, only an infinite present.'[21] His friends considered
such euphoric pronouncements the words of a 'mystic' but, more
recently, Klein has been identified as a precocious postmodernist.[22]
This is not only because of his liberal usage of pastiche as an aesthetic strategy, but because of his fetishization of the present. In
the early 1950s, rather than languishing over the disappearance
of history or positing the deadening totality of the simulacral
present, as the critics Fredric Jameson and Jean Baudrillard
would do in the 1980s, Klein celebrated the possibility of a
perpetual present. Interestingly he not only located its potential
in colour but in language. As his Madrid diary suggests, he was
dreaming of a plan to suppress the past and future tenses. 'I could
abolish the torture of studying in grammar the different tenses
of verbs, regular and irregular. I am determined to put all that
I write as well as all that I say, in the present.'[23] As for judo, he

drew upon advice given to him by an instructor in England to elaborate the notion of an infinite present: 'Movement, life, what we possess in order to act at the bosom of the universe is a constant force: slow, straight, and infallible. It is, if I do not deceive myself, the infinite.'[24] If they would soon become the conceptual manifesto for his monochromes, at the time these motley associations interlacing colour, space and time were the excited daydreams of a 23-year-old whose only vocation was that of a temporary judo instructor.

In June 1951 Fred, Marie and Rose came to visit Klein in Madrid and spent around ten days touring Spain. Klein delegated his job at Bushido Kwai to Arman and travelled by steamship to France via the Balearic Islands. After a summer in Nice and a trip to Italy with his aunt, he joined his parents in Paris, where he stayed until the summer of 1952. This period was difficult for Klein – his mother's fame had grown considerably after she won the Kandinsky Prize in 1949 and her Monday-night salons were attracting artists, critics and art dealers whose budding accomplishments made him reflect on his own unfocused state of affairs. Nevertheless, 'Marie's son', as he was known to her circle of friends, was in regular attendance at his mother's gatherings and, we may surmise, probably heard about (if not saw) the chief exhibitions in Paris that year. These included a show devoted to American Abstract Expressionism entitled *Regards sur la peinture américaine*, organized by Leo Castelli and Sidney Janis at the Galerie de France (February–March 1952) and a solo exhibition of Jackson Pollock's paintings at Studio Fachetti (March 1952). Though he claimed to be 'bored by all this',[25] Klein's confrontation with Abstract Expressionism, as the latest artistic current, provoked a flurry of writing in which it is possible to observe a growing fascination with the rapport between colour and emotion. In another poem, composed as a diary entry, colour becomes a barometer of Klein's mood:

The day is blue
Silence is green
Life is yellow
Light traces
Lines and does not finish again
And me, I linger
Transfixed by indifference!

Soon enough, he extended these reflections to the way other people interact with colours. An undistributed questionnaire poses the following questions:

What does the color Blue, Red, Yellow represent for you? . . .
Which is the most powerful of the three? . . . Which is the
weakest? . . . Which is the most agreeable to look at? . . .
Does the sight of one of these colors in a pure state arouse
any feeling?[26]

Klein's musings did not induce him to create monochromes but they did crystallize his interest in the creative potential of eliding colour with psychological states and, most important, experiencing that melange through vision.

Klein also renewed a friendship with François Dufrêne, whom he had first met at a dinner party in 1950, and was most probably introduced through him to the charismatic agitator Guy Debord. At the time, both men were associated with Isidore Isou's Lettrist group and Klein boasted that he knew people who had shown films at Cannes.[27] He could have been referring to Isou, who had won the avant-garde award for *Traité de Bave et d'éternité* (*Treatise on Venom and Eternity*) in 1951, or to Gil J. Wolman, who screened *Anti-Concept* in February 1952, or to his most intimate friend among the Lettrists, François Dufrêne, who showed *Tambour du jugement premier* (*Drum of First Judgement*) in April 1952. According to Guy Debord's recollections, Klein attended the premier of his imageless film *'Hurlements en faveur de Sade'* (*Howls for Sade*) at the ciné-club Avant-Garde on 30 June 1952.[28] The film, which begins with the words 'Like lost children we live our unfinished lives', consists of 24 minutes of silence followed by a black screen. In true avant-garde style it caused a riot, with boos, shouts and rotten vegetables thrown from the balcony; because of these disruptions it was not shown in its entirety until four months later. Curiously the film's only words resonated with Klein's sentiment of living a prolonged adolescence and his anxiety at being unable to commit to a specific path. 'I am a little afraid', he revealed to Aunt Rose, 'to be so hesitant before life, to be still and always in so much doubt.'[29]

Klein's encounter with Lettrism may have been short-lived but it was consequential. It was not only his earliest association with artists of his generation (other than the personal complicity with Claude Pascal and Arman), but reveals his intellectual proximity to prevailing avant-garde ideas. As Klein's friendship with Dufrêne blossomed, they met for drinks at the La Rotonde bar and discussed their mutual interest in dematerialization. Klein recounts this particularly evocative meeting in 'Some False Foundations, Principles, Etc. And the Condemnation of Evolution', a text he wrote for the first issue of the Lettrist journal *Le Soulèvement de la Jeunesse* (Youth Uprising) in June 1952, at the invitation of Dufrêne. Unlike Klein's diaristic vacillations, this first published work assumes the determined voice of a revolutionary manifesto: He addresses Dufrêne as 'the exalted public educator [of] movies without "film"' and claims that the two of them assembled in 'the same spot where . . . Lenin, thirty years earlier, pondered over the cataclysm of the Russian Revolution'.[30] This heroic inflection is in keeping with the text's broader objective of hailing the radical force of youth. It is linked to Klein's assertion that the 'system of evolution and creation' have different foundations. Evolution, embraced by an older generation, is based on the desire for 'material security'. In contrast, creation is the domain of youth and emerges from the immaterial force of 'enthusiasm'. Klein states that the only way to 'make an intimate revolution is to question everything from a different angle' and that enthusiasm is 'the only means of true and direct investigation'.[31]

With this utopian contribution to the Lettrist journal, Klein was poised to enter Paris's avant-garde circles. Until about 1957 there was a distinct possibility that Klein would be embraced by Guy Debord and the various avant-garde groups that eventually crystallized as the Situationist International in 1957.[32] And while he was ultimately denied because of his 'avowed mysticism', Lettrism greatly influenced his subsequent film production and painterly deliberations.[33] However, in 1952 Klein was still consumed by the polysemic codes of his youth, which made it difficult for him to embrace his parents' bohemian activities or oppose his bourgeois upbringing. Instead his longstanding dream, which grew in scope and intensity after viewing *Howls for Sade*, might be summarized in a succinct sentence from his diary: 'to go to Japan, to study Japanese and Judo, and to make a great oriental documentary as well as a quantity of short film footage of [illegible] and judo courses'.[34] And so Klein busied himself with getting ready for the trip. He began taking classes with Jean Beaujean, a pioneer of the Kodokan method in France who had published a book titled *Ma méthode de judo* (My Judo Method), which Klein owned and annotated. Beaujean had studied with some of the best Japanese masters, including Mikonosuke Kawaishi, and had brought back films through which the Kodokan techniques could be more easily shared and learned. Klein also sat in on Japanese classes at the Ecole des Langues Orientales and devised various schemes in which he figured as an art entrepreneur.[35] In hopes of securing a teaching position he wrote letters to the Japanese cultural attaché in France and to the Franco-Japanese Institute in Tokyo and, through his mother, was introduced to Takachiyo Uemura, an art critic who offered him lodging until he could get settled. Finally, in July 1952, after many months of preparation and with Tantine's support, Klein was able to purchase a ticket to Japan.

No doubt the erratic period between 1948 and 1952 was formative to Klein's process of elaborating a paradoxical lexicon of identities that could not be reducible to a proper name. As he shifted ground between different systems and inclinations, one senses Klein's trepidation in assuming a singular pose. One also gathers his growing interest in the ways that his own image, as both a *judoka* and painter, could potentially intersect. In his journal of 1952 he asks a rhetorical question that he would not be able to answer without taking action: 'Is judo only a con game or a vigorous art?'[36]

3

Assuming the Pose: Yves Klein Fourth *Dan*, 1952–4

I have often been asked if judo played a part in my pictorial conception.
I have until now always answered that it did not. In fact, this is inaccurate:
judo gave me much. I began it almost at the same time as my painting.
One like the other has lived with me like I live with my physical body . . .
Judo has helped me understand that pictorial space is, above all, the
product of spiritual exercises. Judo is, in fact, the discovery of the human
body in spiritual space.[1]

Between 1952 and 1954, Klein's identity crystallized and
disintegrated in dramatic ways. To cultivate the *judoka* persona,
he doggedly tested the categories through which he was perceived
as 'foreigner' or 'native' in both Japan and France. As in all of his
multifaceted identities, this one grew out of a confrontation between
elements whose tensions Klein strategically aggravated. Oscillating
between intense exhilaration and crushing devastation, he reached
the peak of his judo accomplishments with a black belt, fourth *dan*
(level), conferred by the Kodokan Institute, only to begrudgingly
relegate the martial art to a secondary activity. If his gradual
evolution toward art meant a diminished commitment to practising
and teaching judo, years of dedication to the discipline and a free-
form absorption of its Zen philosophy left a permanent mark on
Klein's aesthetic vision.

It should be remembered that Klein's dream of immersing
himself in Japanese culture was highly unusual in the immediate

aftermath of the Second World War and many probably thought that he would never really go on his trip. The country's infrastructure had been devastated and the dropping of atomic bombs on Hiroshima and Nagasaki in 1945 did nothing to make it a popular tourist destination. Following the Yalta Conference, the Allied powers occupied Japan (August 1945–April 1952) and stripped it of its power over Korea, now divided at the 38th Parallel between the Soviet Union and the United States. With the outbreak of conflict between North and South Korea in 1950, the u.s. and United Nations used Japan as a base for military and naval operations that continued through July 1953. Klein was implicated in this political situation only peripherally as the ship on which he sailed to Japan on 22 August 1952, *La Marseillaise*, was transporting UN soldiers to the Korean War. During the month-long ocean crossing, which included stops in Crete, Egypt, Djibouti, Colombo, Singapore, Saigon, Manila and Hong Kong, he eagerly photographed the scenery and posed in front of various monuments. Wearing perfectly creased trousers and a long-sleeved, button-down shirt, there's Klein sitting in a bicycle rickshaw in Singapore and standing in the hubbub of Hong Kong's market. When he finally arrived in Yokohama, his first souvenir was a photograph of the snow-capped Mount Fuji.

Far from home, Klein became more and more aware of his unique position as a judo enthusiast in two different cultural contexts. He notes, for example, that in Paris everyone thought he was pulling their leg when he spoke of going to Japan 'for something as banal as Judo . . . My parents' friends and my own friends scoffed at me for a long time.'[2] More surprising, for Klein, was the lukewarm reception that greeted him when he arrived in Japan, where 'no one can believe that I've come only to study Judo.'[3] Though foreigners regularly came to Tokyo to study at the venerable Kodokan Institute, the premier judo school in Japan, Klein was told that it is not a sport that merits coming so far to learn. 'Everyone tells me, while being greatly entertained, that it's not a sport that one practices when one is young . . . that it's brutal . . . and offers nothing so profound that one should trouble oneself to travel so far.'[4] Despite his years of committed practice, he was regarded as an outsider who could not possibly penetrate judo's spiritual scope and cultural roots. He was evidently aware of his marginalized position. 'Not being Japanese', he writes, 'there's . . . a sort of oriental mysticism that escapes me and that I don't wish to particularly understand.'[5] 'Technically good', according to close friend and judo accomplice Jean Vareilles, Klein was profoundly attracted to performing judo's repetitive sequence of movements, which he described as 'always abstract and purely spiritual' and 'mixing with the passion and emotion of the moment'.[6]

Klein spent the first few weeks living in Yokohama with Takachiyo Uemura, one of the leading Japanese art critics of the post-war period and a good friend of Marie Raymond and Fred Klein. Klein and Uemura saw each other practically every day, and the critic recalls the young man's delight at the habit of local sumo wrestlers who, in place of autographs, would offer their handprint on pieces of cardboard.[7] On 9 October 1952 Klein moved to a small room in Tokyo so that he could be closer to the Kodokan Institute. Much to his frustration, his earlier achievements in France were not recognized and he had to re-ascend the ranks, starting from the lowest grade of white belt. Believing that this was his calling, he followed a gruelling training regime sustained by regular consumption of amphetamines and calcium injections. His exultation is palpable. 'I absolutely must work at this sacred judo and return to France as a great master and champion. It is my future!'[8] Though letters to Aunt Rose may be exaggerated, they suggest that Klein woke up at 7:30am and went to bed at 10pm, with approximately 5 hours of judo practice in between. These sessions took place at both a local club and the Kodokan Institute and Klein complained at having to spend long hours on public transport. As always, the protective familial net was in operation and Rose paid for his tuition and living expenses. Klein also earned some money by teaching at the Franco-Japanese Institute and tutoring two French children. Photographs in his scrapbook document him writing on a blackboard and looking intently at an open book – the perfect image of academic legitimacy. Klein undertook this pedagogical venture rather reluctantly, considering it precious time squandered from judo. The fragmentation between his projected image and inner sentiment is captured by a telling phrase inscribed below these photographs ('I played the role of a teacher and preceptor . . . ').[9]

Klein understood how to exploit the perception of his European extraction to the hilt, yet he gave up this part-time job after four months to devote himself completely to judo. He still needed money and came up with a scheme that involved exporting judo uniforms (*gis*) from Indonesia to France. Unfortunately he neglected to pay the custom fees and had to beg for his aunt's intervention in Marseilles when the shipment of uniforms was held by the Customs Office. On top of this constant financial upkeep, Tantine also made sure her nephew's life was as comfortable as possible by sending him gifts such as pyjamas and an electric razor. Eventually, with her help, he upgraded to living 'in European style' by sharing a room with a fellow judo student named Delange in a neighbourhood close to the British Embassy and having his meals at the Hotel San Bancho.[10] Here, too, Klein projected the image of a well-heeled European, posing by the hotel's swimming pool in his impeccable ensemble. His other extra-curricular activities included organizing exhibitions for his parents at the Franco-Japanese Institute (20–22 February 1953), the Museum of Modern Art in Kamakura (July–August 1953) and the Bridgestone Gallery in Tokyo (3–15 November 1953). In these various enterprises, he continued to capitalize on the cachet of his family's European identity, specifically Marie's and Fred's aesthetic lineage in figuration and abstraction.

While representing his parents' work, Klein became acquainted with the emerging critic Shinichi Segi, who recalls the young man's indifference to the local artistic scene and his all-consuming passion for judo. The one purported episode where Klein may have shown variously coloured monochromes on paper to Segi resulted in 'politeness and silence'.[11] Above all, Klein's mission was to become the titular example of Tokyo-style (Kodokan) judo, return to France shrouded in glory and open his own club. Like a growing number of devotees, Klein considered this method more authentic and pure than the one that had been adopted in France in the 1930s when Master Kawaishi Shihan (from Kyoto) opened the first 'Club Franco Japonais de Jiu-Jitsu' in Paris. With unwavering determination, he repeated his previous achievements and worked his way from white to brown belt. He attained the first *dan*, black belt, on 11 January 1953 and his second *dan* on 16 July 1953.

Klein was convinced that to outshine his competitors in France he would have to secure the fourth *dan*, an extremely difficult feat that would take several years of training. His well-earned judo achievements are hard to separate from an elaborately concocted scheme set in motion after he was refused this grade. A letter to Tantine casts the situation in this way.

I am fed up with this country. I am a nervous wreck and only want one thing: To return to France as soon as possible. But, above all, I want to get what I came here for. I absolutely must obtain the 4th *dan* from the Kodokan . . . I have the reputation of being the best foreign student and all the professors believe that I deserve the 4th even the 5th *dan*. But, alas, they are all more or less anti-foreigners, and they have decided not to give advancement to a foreigner unless he has won it at least ten times over, or if they allow themselves to be tempted by money.[12]

Klein begged his aunt to write to Mr Tashiro, the Secretary General of the Kodokan Institute, and vouch that he had 'three or four million francs' at his disposal to open a judo club in Paris. The 'battle', as he called it, had to be won no matter what and he believed that this 'bluff' would 'produce results'.[13] He also implored his previous judo clubs, in Nice, Madrid and Paris, to confirm that they would make him their 'Technical Director' if the Kodokan were to grant him the fourth *dan*.[14] Rose heeded her nephew's pleas and sent a letter on 18 November 1953. A negative response from Mr Tashiro arrived on 7 December 1953, followed only eleven days later by an overturning of the ruling from Risei Kano, the President of the Kodokan. His reasoning was Klein's 'pure and simple enthusiasm for Judo, [his] coming to Japan – a very distant country geographically, and [his] future project for the cause of developing the true Judo of the Kodokan in Europe'.[15] This incredible sequence of events, which transpired in a brief two-month period, reveals Klein's mastery in activating an identity located at the interstices between East and West. To find a job tutoring French, he cannily occupied the position of 'foreigner', but railed against this same appellation when it came to his treatment at the Kodokan. At the same time, he knew it would be to his advantage to paint himself as an anointed emissary of the method in France and to endear himself as an 'insider' to the Kodokan. Ecstatic at becoming the first 'foreigner' to be granted the fourth *dan*, he retraced his journey on *La Marseillaise*, arriving in Nice in early February 1954.

Not long after his return, on 19 February 1954, Klein presented himself at the French Judo Federation, ready to be bestowed with due distinction. Nothing could have prepared him for the shock of the rejection. He was informed that the grades he had obtained in Japan were not valid and that he would have to pass local exams to prove his abilities. This news was devastating. Until he was recognized by the French Federation, he would not be able to participate in official European championships or teach judo in France. Profoundly wounded, Klein vehemently refused to take further exams and sank into utter dejection. 'It's a catastrophe', he wrote to Tantine, ' . . . I am in complete despair . . . I had hoped to be greeted triumphantly in Paris . . . and am met only by jealousy, envy, and dishonesty.'[16] In Klein's wild speculations, this snub could only have been driven by the Federation's 'fear' at admitting such an 'honest' high-ranked *judoka* who might 'oppose their "power".'[17] Both his parents and aunt tried to exert their influence to reverse this decision but to no avail. Klein's hopes were dashed and he vowed to give up judo in disgust.

It took a couple of months for him to rally from the blow, but it seemed like his luck might be changing when on 17 April 1954 he signed a contract with the venerable Editions Bernard Grasset to write a book on judo. While in Tokyo he had taken countless photographs and began to make a film with a fellow Kodokan student from California named Harold Sharp. Using Sharp's 16mm camera and rare access to celluloid, the two gathered more than 8,000 feet of documentary material, which included demonstrations of judo's basic movements (the *katas*) and a presentation of judo champions performing specific techniques.

> I asked these champions to present each of their specialties in the *uchikomi* form, that is to say, to show their particular manner of preparing and perfecting their movements. Then I filmed them executing these movements in combat with different adversaries in order to show all their opportunities and 'moments'.[18]

Using this extensive documentation, Klein prepared an illustrated guide to the six *katas* that formed the basis of the Kodokan method. *Les Fondements du Judo* (The Fundamentals of Judo) includes 50 sketches and 375 photographs and was touted as bringing 'the true

Japanese method' to Europe. The preface, written by Ichiro Abe, a high-ranking Kodokan representative, praised Klein for filling 'a great hole in European literature on Judo'.[19] If he had been a 'foreigner' in Japan, Klein now became the country's greatest ambassador in Europe. The 'native son's' answer to the French Federation's painful rejection was to become the resident embodiment of Kodokan judo.

Klein also had great plans for an experimental film project that went unrealized. In an unpublished essay by Takachiyo Uemura titled 'Yves Klein in Tokyo', written in November 1960, the Japanese critic claims that Klein wished to convert judo movements into 'abstract animated lines or imprints traced directly onto the film'.[20] Though attempts to secure funding from the Japanese Cinematography Society were unsuccessful, Klein still had the project in mind in 1954 when he drafted a letter to Jean Cocteau asking him to direct the film and draft a screen-play. A short résumé of the film, provisionally titled 'Draft for a Scenario no. 1 – Judo', describes it as having 'a length of 1500 meters (about 60 minutes or even double this)', and aiming to 'dis-engage the poetic formulas from different Japanese sports'.[21] Like many of Klein's precocious ideas, this one fell by the wayside. Nevertheless, it points to his awareness of contemporary avant-garde film practices in Paris, where members of the Lettrist group were deconstructing the basic conventions and support structures of film.

Klein could not officially practise judo without the Federation's authorization, which rendered him a performer without a stage. Neither drinks with François Dufrêne in Montparnasse nor the Renault 4 cv that his aunt bought him offered any consolation. In May 1954, at the invitation of Fernando Franco de Sarabia and with Claude Pascal (who was recovering from tuberculosis) in tow, Klein drove from Nice to Madrid and started teaching at his old friend's club: the Bushido Kwai. He also became the technical advisor of the Spanish Judo Federation and travelled to Barcelona, San Sebastian, Valencia and other cities to give demonstrations of the Kodokan technique. While in Spain, did Klein also train General Francisco Franco's Civil Guard? Was it a case of misguided bravado, convenient pecuniary gain, or a fanciful invention on the part of the artist? There are discrepant accounts about Klein's involvement with Franco's police force, a controversial accusation that has haunted his posthumous reception and continues to pose interpretive dilemmas for those who would like to narrate Klein's biography as being free of paradoxes or contradictions. It is important to note that the different version of events surrounding this sensitive topic stem from testimonies offered by two of Klein's closest friends and colleagues, Pierre Restany and Claude Pascal, who were interviewed individually in the early 1980s in preparation for groundbreaking exhibitions in Houston (1982) and Paris (1983). Of the two, it is Restany who appears more assured in stating that 'In Madrid, Yves Klein was a judo instructor in the Civil Guard. He was attached to a department charged with the personal security of Franco during the year '54', and noting that Jean Lafon, who would become co-manager of the brasserie La Coupole in 1960, 'knew Yves Klein in Madrid. He was doing a formation in hotel management. He could confirm the fact. Yves' reputation of being a Fascist comes from there.[22] Pascal, on the other hand, speculates that Klein completely fabricated the story as an expedient excuse to leave Spain. 'I know that he had had enough. He must have searched [for an excuse] for his Aunt . . . maybe he invented [it] . . . to scare his Aunt who became afraid easily. "I have an issue with the Civil Guard."'[23] While we may never know quite what happened in Madrid in 1954, it appears that Klein's main focus was on practising judo at any cost and regardless of political affiliations. His return to Spain is one of those paradoxical moments during which he unequivocally voiced his support for 'the veritable age of judo's colonization in Europe' while also taking decisive steps toward an artistic practice with the publication of *Yves Peintures* and *Hagenault Peintures* in November 1954.[24]

Klein's time in Madrid came to an end when he became embroiled in another heated argument regarding his status as a *judoka*. Using the 'bluff' technique he believed had succeeded in Japan, he tried to attain a superior position with the Spanish Judo Federation, only to be definitively rebuffed. He returned to Paris despondent as ever, berating the sport that had caused him so much chagrin. 'It's finished', he wrote to Tantine, 'I am abandoning [judo] and will become a bum if necessary . . . I have no more illusions about this dirty joke of judo.'[25] His sense of failure was overwhelming. To his family, he grumbled that he would spend Christmas all alone ('tout seul!') – without parents, aunt, or anyone else. The brunt of his wrath was directed at the Kodokan Institute, whom he blamed for not supporting him as the representative of their method in Europe. At his wits' end, he wrote a letter to the director of the Kodokan, attributing his defeat in Spain to a cabal run by 'crooks' and ascribing his powerlessness to his situation as a 'foreigner' in Madrid.[26]

To put it mildly, Klein's return from Japan did not turn out the way he had expected and the end of 1954 found him in a bad way. Sitting at the Café Select in Montparnasse, he confided to his diary, 'I am in search of something big. I have realized that one can also find pleasure in pride. I think I am a genius yet I don't produce anything sensational.'[27] No matter how depressed he may have been, he was not fully ready to renounce the *judoka* persona. In December 1954 he attended the European judo championships in Brussels with his friend Sarabia and delivered his manuscript to Editions Grasset. Klein enjoyed the ensuing book signings and boasted of his television appearance. At the end of 1954 a chance encounter with Charles-Henri Le Moing, a member of the American Center for Students and Artists on the boulevard Raspail, led to Klein's recruitment as a judo instructor for a newly formed club in the institution's basement. Klein signed an exclusive contract on 23 February 1955 and taught the Kodokan method to beginner and advanced students at the American Center until 15 December 1959. Through the club, Klein became acquainted with Robert Godet – fourth *dan*, founder of the International Federation of Judo, adept of George Gurdjieff's esoteric teachings and international man of mystery. Godet had been a liaison agent in the Resistance and many suspected that his job as the representative of Bordeaux wines in Southeast Asia was only a front to cover for a weapon-smuggling operation. With mutual devotion to occult beliefs and intrigue, it is easy to see why Godet and Klein became fast friends, despite a significant age difference. They remained close until Godet died in a plane crash in 1960, apparently on a mission to supply guns to Tibetan guerillas battling the Chinese army.

In 1955, with his family's assistance, Klein finally became the owner and director of his own club, Judo Académie de Paris. Located at 104 boulevard de Clichy in Montmartre, the club opened in late September or early October 1955. A publicity poster hails Klein as 'Black Belt, 4th Dan, Graduate of the Kodokan of Tokyo' and shows him performing a judo manoeuvre. It also advertises classes for children and beginners, the study of the *katas* and projections of Klein's judo films. The club attracted neighbourhood youths and adults, but Klein was forced to close it only a year later, in the summer of 1956, because of insufficient enrolment. During its year of operation, Klein used the club's walls to display blue, white and rose monochromes, each 7 to 8 metres long. More than just a convenient backdrop, Klein's gradually intertwining dedication to judo and painterly abstraction merits greater scrutiny. According to art historian Mark Cheetham, 'the canvas and judo mat were interchangeable.'[28] This elision emerged from Klein's espousal of Kodokan-style judo, which led him to consider art practice 'holistic' rather than 'pure' or 'autonomous'.[29] Steeped in Zen thought, he approached judo as 'the discovery by the human body of spiritual space'.[30] For Cheetham, this attitude motivated Klein to attempt 'dynamic levitation' in the performance known as *Leap Into The Void* (1960) and to use nude women as paint-smearing 'live brushes' in the *Anthropometries* (1960). In all of these actions, the artist's goal was to negate formal boundaries, break down conventional hierarchies and merge categories, spaces and experiences. Yet as Cheetham rightfully cautions, Klein's art did not just subsume the principles of judo *in toto*. Rather, the 'monochrome, Rosicrucianism, *and* judo . . . mixed to form a somehow consistent life as artwork'.[31]

On a par with all of Klein's other activities, judo was a practice and a way of life through which he simultaneously produced effects of identity that oscillated between privilege and populism, insider and outsider, Western tourist and Eastern mystic. Even after closing his judo academy and giving notice at the American Center, he never stopped practising judo on his own.

4

'Painter', 1954–5

> I want to 'be,' plain and simple. I will be a 'painter.' People will say of
> me: that's the 'painter.' And I will feel myself to be a 'painter,' a true
> one precisely because I won't paint or at least not in appearance. The
> fact that I 'exist' as a painter will be my most 'formidable' pictorial
> work of the present age.[1]

Yves Klein became a 'painter' in the same year as Henri Matisse's
death. The famous master passed away in Nice on 3 November
1954 while Klein was still in Madrid. During the last years of his
life, Matisse produced paper cutouts, including the *Blue Nude*
series (1950–54), a double homage to the colour blue and the
female form that profoundly affected Klein in ways that would
become visible a few years later, most notably by activating the
blue nude as a living 'brush'. Between 1954 and 1955, however,
the *judoka* was still making tentative steps toward art practice
and, more specifically, in the direction of his parents' métier. The
son of Fred Klein and Marie Raymond, who had long shunned his
bohemian rearing, shrewdly launched himself in the Parisian art
scene by assuming the persona of a 'painter'. Adopting his parents'
painterly styles or operating according to the criteria that validated
their talent was out of the question. More radically, he was interested
in the discursive field *surrounding* painting rather than in replicating
its accepted conventions. Klein's fascination was less in representing
the world through figuration or abstraction, the dominant painterly

languages in the immediate post-war period; following Marcel Duchamp, Klein was keen to expose how specific artistic and social conventions validated an artwork as a painting. He went about revealing the subtle legitimizing mechanisms, which were generally accepted as universal truths, through a two-pronged strategy: by calling on the history and conventions of the medium (as proof of his painterly integrity) while also explicitly parodying them (to reveal the variable norms through which painting gains meaning at a particular time and place).

Though the date of Klein's first dated art objects is still contested, it would be safe to say that he launched the 'painter' persona with the publication of *Yves Peintures* and *Hagenault Peintures* on 18 November 1954. These two sets of conceptually charged catalogues (each 24.4 cm x 19.7 cm) were fabricated in the printing shop of Sarabia's father in Jaen, near Madrid, with the financial assistance of Aunt Rose. They were printed in an edition of 150 numbered copies on high-grade paper and contained ten variously coloured monochromatic plates made of commercially inked paper. A three-page preface by 'Pascal Claude' consists of typographical lines arranged horizontally to imitate paragraphs of text. A mechanically reproduced signature, which attributed the plates to 'Yves', was included on some, but not all, of the plates, along with a caption marking the capital city of each work's production (Paris, Madrid, London, Tokyo, Nice). Some captions also provide the work's dimensions (without noting which system of measurement is used) and a credit line that cites the work's attribution: 'Collection Particulière' (Private Collection), 'Appartient à l'auteur (Belongs to the Author), 'Collection Raymond Hains'. A supposed inventory of mono-chromes produced during his international peregrinations of the late 1940s and early '50s, these enigmatic works to which the catalogue makes reference did not physically exist at the time, nor would they ever exist in this form.

The brilliance of Klein's opening salvo was his construction of an artistic persona through a wry critique of the conventions through which an artist is publicly endowed with an aura of authenticity. To become a 'painter', he wouldn't actually have to go through the difficult exercise of producing tangible objects, but only create the 'effect' that he'd abided by the accepted procedures of 'painting'. Appearance would not simply precede reality but would actually construct it. This strategy is launched with the playfulness of the works' laconic titles – *Yves Peintures* (*Yves Paintings*) introduces the monosyllabic artist as a trademark coupled with his medium of choice. *Hagenault Peintures* (*Hagenault Paintings*), meanwhile, replaces the artist's Christian name with that of a mass-produced variety of fruit cake popular in France in the 1950s and links this readymade to his artwork. With all three terms ('Yves', 'Hagenault' and 'Peintures') Klein offered himself to the public as a non-threatening brand available for immediate consumption.

At the same time, he critically de-familiarized the act, meaning and conventions of painting. Though an author's name accompanies the preface (Claude Pascal spelled backwards), Klein deconstructed the conventions of original authorship by supplying purely graphic 'text' that withholds rather than illuminates meaning. The well-regimented, horizontal lines may signify 'writing' and the public may be invited to 'read' the 'text', but none of the protocols of narratives can be used to decode the sequence of mute marks. Through this minimalist gesture, Klein affirms and mocks the habitual custom of including a preface by a well-known critic or philosopher to explain and validate an artist's work. And if a catalogue is traditionally published to document works that the artist has already fabricated and exhibited, Klein's drolly offered reproductions of paintings that do not yet exist. 'Yves', the unknown artist, who had yet to create a cohesive body of work, reverses the steps of the typical art career by showing copies before originals.

Without alluding to Marcel Duchamp in any explicit way, he embraced the readymade as the very condition of possibility for post-war artistic practice.

As noted by the art historian Denys Riout, Klein's catalogues are also reminiscent of the late nineteenth-century folio of Alphonse Allais.[2] The French humorist, who was affiliated with the Montmartre cabaret Le Chat-Noir, first exhibited his 'Monochroidals' at the Salon of Incoherent Arts in 1883. Published in 1897, his chef d'oeuvre is the *Album primo-avrilesque*, a small book that parodied the contemporaneous meanings of colour and line. Fifty-seven years before Klein's espousal of reductive abstraction, Allais presented seven full-page displays of 'Monochroidals', the name he gave to his monochromatic plates. Each uniformly coloured plate was set within a decorative frame and accompanied by a satirical title. Mocking the symbolist poets and their fervour for synthesthetic correspondences, Allais titled the blue plate 'Stupor of Young Recruits Noticing for the First Time Your Azure, Oh Mediterranean Sea!' In a similar vein, the album concludes with a two-page 'Funeral March' ('especially composed for the funerals of a great deaf man') consisting of empty music staves that suggest the inability of linear notation to capture sound. Are Klein's catalogues an homage or a spoof of Allais' album? Did he even know about them? Though separated by more than half a century, both artists employed parody as a way to reveal the function of line and colour as purveyors of meaning. To become 'Yves Le Monochrome' (Yves the Monochrome), one might expect that Klein would condense his identity to the singular element of colour. Yet, as he would show time and again, his identity could never be bound to a sole component but was constructed from the perpetual appropriation and irritation of multiple categories. In *Yves Peintures* and *Hagenault Peintures*, colour and line are equally vital parts in the constitution and presentation of the artist's persona.

Klein realized that to become a 'painter' required more than projecting his intention to the public; it also entailed soliciting their response. His persona crystallized at the intersection between intention and reception in a zone where the mutual expectations of artist and public chafed against each other. While the horizontal lines that comprise the preface to the catalogues do not communicate anything beyond their own graphic identity and the plates do not represent 'original' paintings, Klein is aware that line (as text) and colour (as image) are forms of address to both existing and imagined publics. He takes great care to rebuff the deep-rooted expectations of how line and colour should 'properly' signify. This is not fraudulence or insincerity on Klein's part. By conditioning viewers to apprehend familiar conventions in different ways, he sets the stage for a public that is yet-to-come. Though his ambitions were still tilted towards judo, he incorporated fact and fiction, original and copy, sincerity and parody, to articulate the persona for a different kind of 'painter', one for which there was no contemporaneous conceptual vocabulary.

In early December 1954, shortly after the catalogues' publication, Klein returned from Spain to France and, with no clear prospects, lapsed into another bout of malaise. With his family's financial support, he opened his own judo studio, but the possibility of gaining recognition as a painter was becoming more and more tantalizing. Klein's entrée into artistic circles was greatly facilitated by his parents' stature in the Parisian scene. Yet for all their clout with the Ecole de Paris, 'Marie's son' was more interested in meeting the younger generation of artists who made Montparnasse their home. By frequenting neighbourhood bistros and cafés he became friendly with Jean Tinguely, Jacques Villeglé and Raymond Hains, artists who subsequently became part of the Nouveau Réaliste group. He also forged friendships with Jacques Polieri, an up-and-coming scenographer, Edouard Adam, owner of the local art supply store, and Rodolphe Pichon, a tailor who dressed young artists free of charge. Klein began visiting Pichon's studio on the rue Campagne-Première, a narrow street burgeoning with artists' ateliers, where he met César, Sam Szafran and Bernard Quentin. Through Robert Godet, he was introduced to more established figures such as the Count Arquian, who directed the Galerie Internationale d'Art Contemporain, and to young collectors searching for new talent. Perhaps most importantly, Godet also presented Klein to Bernadette Allain, who was swiftly named 'Baba', a young architect who became his steady girlfriend, intellectual interlocutor, judo companion and, for many years, unacknowledged collaborator.

In 1955 Klein began producing an eclectic collection of monochromes in a variety of colours, canvas sizes and surface textures. Since the habitual path to being recognized as a serious painter was to submit a work to one of the Salons, Klein presented a matte-orange painting titled *Expression de l'univers de la couleur mine orange* (*Expression of the World of the Color Lead-Orange)* to the Salon des Réalités Nouvelles in May 1955. Founded only nine years earlier, this Salon was devoted to exhibiting abstract work and had been a regular forum for Marie Raymond's paintings from its inception. Much to Klein's surprise and indignation, his flawless orange monochrome – whose uniform surface was interrupted only by his initials and the date – was refused by the Salon's committee on 5 July 1955. Like the rejection of Marcel Duchamp's *Fountain* from the exhibition of the Society of Independent Artists in 1917, Klein's collision with the jury revealed that he was a threat to the dominant artistic criteria.

Most significant in Klein's written account is the way he crafts the persona of a 'painter' from the discourse surrounding the event rather than the particular quality of his painting. His text, a masterful work of fiction, reveals a canny exploitation of the conflict. In the first section, he specifies the criteria used by the Salon:

In 1955, I register during the required period, after having specified to the secretariat that I am not at all figurative . . . and after having showed some photos (I am told that it will perhaps be difficult to make a good print from the photos for the catalogue). They accept my fee and register me. Some months later, I receive notice to bring my entry to the hanging in the Palais des Beaux Arts de la Ville de Paris.[3]

This rather nonchalant prologue has Klein easily meeting the bureaucratic requirements (entering by the due date and paying the required fee) and fulfilling the aesthetic criteria (presenting non-figurative work) without a hitch. In the second section Klein hints at slight cracks in the jury's consensus over what constitutes 'abstraction' but the bureaucracy maintains a veneer of harmony. He writes,

There, in front of my canvas, various members of the committee who are present hesitate a moment, but agree quite rapidly, with a sort of 'Oui, of course,' that it's all right. They then give me a receipt in exchange and store my painting, which I have titled *Expression du monde de la couleur mine orange*.[4]

If the jury and the artist appear to be in basic agreement, Klein quickly shifts the tone of the narrative in the next section as he lays the groundwork for the impending rupture: 'The next afternoon, I receive a very curt letter announcing the refusal to exhibit me, and asking me to come as quickly as possible to take away my canvas "for want of space to store refused entries." Such is the brutal tone of the letter.'[5] Heightening the drama, Klein responds to the committee's decision with a letter of protest in which he assures them of his 'sincere and serious intentions, fearing perhaps that they thought it was a provocative joke in bad taste on [his] part'.[6] He continues to amplify the stakes by recounting a telephone conversation between the committee and his mother in which the divergent positions are articulated. 'You understand,' they tell Marie Raymond, 'it is really not enough, but if Yves would agree at least to add a small line, or a point, or even simply a touch of another color, we would be able to hang it. But only one uniform color, no, no. Truly, this is not enough, it is impossible.'[7]

Klein categorically refused to change any aspect of his work and was politely yet definitively rejected from the Salon. An unpublished text reveals that his retribution was to send about 50 of his friends to the opening to protest his exclusion. They 'madly tapped their feet on the ground and shouted, "No, no, no, it will not be hung, no, no, no!"'[8] Though the divisive issue seemed to revolve over the nature of abstraction, the stand-off between Klein and the Salon jury ultimately revealed that aesthetic consensus is not universal but emerges from a host of bureaucratic decisions and institutional procedures. By satirizing the sequence of events, Klein made the committee appear like conservative buffoons and framed himself as a misunderstood painter too advanced for his times. This account is a riveting example of Klein's profound understanding that his identity as a 'painter' would not simply be constituted by his artistic oeuvre but in the forum of public opinion too.

Following this insight, Klein began a small campaign to invite critics to see his work. He had little success, yet an earnest letter to Jacques Tournier betrays Klein's awareness of the criticism that awaited him. 'You will tell me that my uni-colored paintings are too easily imitable and that everyone can make them . . . Not everybody can spread paint on a canvas in a satisfactory manner with a brush, roller, or even a gun without the necessary culture and technical knowledge.'[9] Despite these prognostics, there was one person who did not turn Klein away: the young critic Pierre Restany.

5

Avant-garde Artist, 1955–7

The position of MALEVICH in relation to me makes it possible to leave by
the static speed of the immeasurable spirit of the phenomenology of time
and allows me to say honestly and calmly that MALEVICH painted a still
life based on one of my monochrome paintings.[1]

The rejection from the Salon des Réalités Nouvelles was a turning
point in Klein's self-construction. When the Salon snubbed his
orange monochrome, a petition of protest began to circulate in
Paris's art world and was signed, as a matter of principle, by a
wide spectrum of individuals. Though this did not alter the jury's
decision, his name was now indelibly associated with a posture
of recalcitrance. Just like those rebuffed from the official Salon of
1863, who subsequently gained notoriety at the Salon des Refusés,
Klein realized the power that came with contesting the institution of
art from within its own parameters. Why settle for being a 'painter'
when he could also tap into the transgressive cachet that came with
being an 'avant-gardiste'? With this in mind, between 1955 and 1957
Klein took every possible step to deploy the strategies of earlier
avant-gardes and oppose the values, conventions and systems of
power through which bourgeois society represented itself. As he
provoked the very same establishment to which he desperately
wanted to belong, Klein's career spectacularly blossomed.

The first of these wilful aggravations occurred on 15 October
1955 at the Club des Solitaires, located at 121 avenue de Villiers in

the seventeenth arrondissement. As anticipated, Klein benefited from his parents' connections to secure this venue, a showroom housed in the same building as the publishing enterprise of Editions Lacoste, where he displayed about twenty variously coloured monochromes. The exhibition, titled *Yves Peintures* (Yves Paintings), was accompanied by a text that Klein had adapted from his letter to the critic Jacques Tournier. In it, he romantically extolled the potency of uniform colour to evoke a spectrum of emotions. 'For me,' he writes, 'each nuance of color is, in some way, an individual ... There are nuances that are gentle, mad, violent, majestic, vulgar, calm, etc.'[2] In a roundabout way, Klein also addressed his recent experience at the Salon des Réalités Nouvelles, in which his participation hinged on adding a stylistic element to an otherwise uniform orange surface. With *carte blanche* to have the final word, Klein insisted on his interest in 'abstract concepts represented in an abstract matter' but took a jab at abstract painters who 'reproach' him for 'refusing to juxtapose colors and provoke relationships among them'.[3] Despite such strategic goading, the opening did not attract a significant attendance; collectors, gallery owners and critics had yet to accept Klein as a serious artist and the exhibition location was too remote for unprompted visits.

Knowing full well that he had to heighten his visibility, Klein referred to his debut as an 'Exhibition of Contact'.[4] The idea was to rub shoulders with as many people as possible and secure another exhibition. The prevailing reaction from the few who took the time to see the show was derision and, to all intents and purposes, Klein accomplished what he had set out to do. Although he did not achieve either the *succès de scandal* or the *succès d'estime* for which he may have hoped, this sharp public response piqued the interest of Pierre Restany, whose visit to the exhibition changed the course of both their lives.

Born in 1930 in the small village of Amélie-les-Bains in the Pyrenees, Restany spent his childhood in Casablanca, where his father was a prominent businessman and loyal supporter of General Charles de Gaulle. In 1949 he began his studies at the prestigious Lycée Henri IV in Paris and took preparatory courses to be admitted to the Ecole Nationale d'Adminstration. After two failed attempts to pass the entry examination, Restany enrolled in the university in Pisa, where he studied art history and Italian, and participated in an eighteen-month academic exchange in Ireland during which he researched illuminated manuscripts. He had always been gifted in languages, had composed poetry from an early age and had an astonishing knowledge of literature, but this scholastic detour was the spark that ignited his passion for the arts. Unwillingly he returned to France at his father's insistence in 1953, and accepted a job drafting documents and reports for the Ministry of Public Works, Transportation and Tourism. This day job as a civil servant, which made him financially solvent, enabled Restany to follow his calling and soon he was a staple of the emerging abstract art scene, which congregated around the Galerie Fachetti in the heart of Saint-Germain-des-Prés. His earliest criticism appeared in the French journals *Libre Propos*, *Preuves* and *Symphonie* and the Italian revue *Quattro Soli*, and his first exhibition essays accompanied the work of young artists such as Claude Bellegarde and René Laubiès. In 1954 Restany was invited to join the cabinet of the Gaullist politician Jacques Chaban-Delmas. Had he desired a career in politics, this esteemed post, which had him writing ministerial speeches, could have served as an important stepping stone. But Restany's heart was not it in and he continued to travel across Europe and meet artists, such as Nam June Paik and John Cage, and befriend gallery owners, such as Jean-Pierre Wilhelm and Guido Le Noci.[5]

Restany's emergence as an influential critic was rooted in his exceptional rhetorical skills, polemical acuity and unwavering commitment to art. It was also connected to the deficiencies in the contemporaneous field of criticism, which did not yet have a local spokesperson for the up-and-coming generation of cultural producers. In the mid-1950s there were only a handful of Parisian critics and each one had laid claim to a specific group of artists or style of painting. The aristocratic Michel Tapié de Céléyran (1907–1987) represented artists associated with the strain known as Lyrical Abstraction, among them Georges Mathieu, Camille Bryen, Hans Hartung and Wols. Meanwhile, Charles Estienne (1908–1966), a contributor to the left-wing journal *Combat* and a partisan of Surrealism, backed artists who displayed an 'abstract surrealism' such as Jean Messagier and René Duvillier. Another critic to *Combat* and one of the only women writers of note was Claude Rivière (b. 1932), who defended mostly young, unknown artists and who was a supporter of Iris Clert's stable. The fourth figure was Michel Ragon (b. 1924), who promoted proletarian writers, poets of the Resistance and anarchists during the Second World War before turning his attention to the visual arts. Ragon, too, was a proponent of abstraction, including painters such as Hans Hartung, Gérard Schneider, Pierre Soulages and the international avant-garde group COBRA. The last significant critical voice was that of Julien Alvard (1916–1974), the editor of the journal *Cimaise*, who was more inclined toward painters of the 'grande tradition' such as Claude Monet. Based on this preference for Impressionism, he launched a movement called 'nuagisme' (Cloudism), which included artists such as René Laubies, Frédéric Benrath, Fernando Lerin and Nasser Assar.

Pierre Restany joined the ranks of these French critics when he began to support the work of the young avant-garde artist Yves Klein. With Arman as an intermediary, the two met on 1 December 1955 after Restany saw Klein's monochromes at the Club de Solitaires. Their meeting began with coffee at a shabby café on the rue du Bac in Saint-Germain, continued with lunch at the Ministry's caféteria, and ended with an outing that same evening.[6] Klein came with a clear goal: to convince Restany to write a text for an exhibition at a gallery owned by his parents' friend, Colette Allendy. Four years after the death of her husband, René Allendy, a prominent psychoanalyst and one of the founding members of Société psychanalytique de Paris, Colette Allendy had transformed the two rooms on the ground floor of her private house on the rue d'Assomption in the sixteenth arrondissement into an exhibition space. Since its opening in 1946 the Galerie Colette Allendy had built a solid reputation, with an eclectic roster representing both the older generation of artist, such as Sonia Delaunay, Paul Klee and Francis Picabia, and current trends such as Lyrical Abstraction and Art Informel. Fondly referred to by Restany as 'the gallery for desperate causes', this space became a breeding ground for a cross-generational group of avant-garde artists.[7] After Klein's debut failed to spark the immediate triumph that he expected, he approached Allendy with a few monochromes in hand in an attempt to win her over. Not entirely convinced by the young man's talents but afraid to turn Marie Raymond's son away, she found a diplomatic solution. She would show Klein's paintings only if he could persuade a recognized critic to introduce his work. Faced with this conundrum and a nagging feeling that this was his last chance to launch his artistic career, Klein came to Restany in the hope that he would be his 'patron'. Struck by Klein's charisma and singular ideas on colour, Restany agreed and, as promised, Allendy scheduled a solo exhibition for the following year. This pact between artist and critic kindled a lifelong, mutually beneficial relationship.

With this important event fast approaching, Klein worked feverishly in his judo studio, which still doubled as his atelier. He was in search of the perfect hue with a 'brilliance and an extraordinary, autonomous life of [its] own', which meant long hours at Edouard Adams' supply store, extensive conversations about perception and colour with Bernadette Allain and endless experiments with different ratios of paint, thinner and binder.[8]

Unable to attain a 'medium capable of fixing the pure pigment to the support without altering it', he turned to the expertise of engineers at the industrial corporation Rhône-Poulenc.[9] The company produced a special fixative sold under the name Rhodopas M or M60A. It was composed of ethyl alcohol, ethyl acetate and vinyl chloride resin and, although it was extremely toxic, enabled Klein to fabricate paintings with a shimmering, powdery surface.[10] Klein was working down to the wire, three days before the opening of *Yves: Propositions monochromes* (21 February–7 March 1956), an exhibition comprised of twenty monochromes in different formats and colours. It was a daring stance at a time when the habitual canvas was a strict rectangle and no other artist in Paris was taking abstraction to its logical conclusion by presenting uniformly coloured paintings. His finishing touch, which became a leitmotif for all his monochromes, was to slightly round the edges of each canvas and paint it in the same colour as the surface. He also started to sign many of his paintings with the moniker 'yves le monochrome' (yves the monochrome).

Restany's text, *La Minute de Verité* (The Minute of Truth), championed the radicality of Klein's monochromes by claiming that each one of his 'propositions' defined a 'visual field, a colored space, which has eliminated all graphical inscriptions and has thus escaped duration'.[11] Restany differentiated Klein's paintings from historical precedents (such as Kasimir Malevich) and contemporary examples of abstraction (that is, Lyrical Abstraction and Art Informel) by arguing for its 'strictly objective' nature.[12] Having eliminated all mark-making, figure-ground relationships and decorative aspects that might liken them to murals, Klein's monochromes offered something completely new. Restany argued that 'for all those intoxicated by the machine and the big city, to those frenzied by rhythm and masturbated by reality, Yves offers a cure of silence.'[13] In contrast to the external contamination that shaped other forms of abstraction, Restany hailed Klein's paintings as autonomous phenomena capable of arousing 'pure contemplation' in the spectator.[14]

This flurry of exaggerated prose and promise of a quasi-transcendental experience flamed interest in the exhibition and Klein organized a public debate at the gallery on 2 March 1956 to meet the curious and address the critics. An article by Bernadette Allain reveals the public's confusion about Klein's intentions and the mystification through which his avant-gardiste persona was formed. In keeping with the historically contentious relation between the avant-garde and the bourgeois public, some asked whether Klein made the monochromes in 'the spirit of provoca-tion' and, if so, why he would put so much time into a 'studied lack of deference toward the public'.[15] Other queries broached Klein's Japanese influences, especially his knowledge of single-panel screens, and his relation to architectonic painting, which in the spirit of Bauhaus and Le Corbusier integrated single-colour panels into buildings.[16] Klein was most troubled by the public's tendency not to engage with each painting individually but respond to the installation *relationally* and thus 'recreate decorative and architec-tural elements out of the colors'.[17] He believed that this flawed reception of his work stemmed from the public's preconceived ways of looking at abstract art. The failure to communicate his intent meant one thing: the public would have to be taught new ways of looking and seeing. Yet even Klein could not free himself from Western conventions of bourgeois subjectivity as he dubbed each 'nuance of a color . . . an individual, a being that is of the same race as the basic color but clearly possesses a unique character, and a distinct, personal soul'.[18] Despite the mixed reactions, Klein's solo exhibition at the Galerie Colette Allendy was a turning point in his career.

His personal life was also taking an unexpected twist. A serendipitous encounter occurred when Marcel Barillon de

Murat visited Allendy's gallery. He was a Knight in the Order of St Sebastian, a Catholic group founded in France in 1452 to protect the relics of St Sebastian at the Abbey of St Médard in Soissons, which had been revived in 1952 by the anointment of a new Grand Master after half a century of dormancy. The separation between Church and State under the constitution of the French Republic meant that the Order had a largely ceremonial role, but with its elaborate rituals and colourful regalia (including a sword and ostrich-plumed, three-cornered hat) it could not have been more appropriate for Klein. His taste for adventure, Catholic upbringing, initiation into the Cult of St Rita and fascination with Rosicrucianism very naturally led him to the Order of St Sebastian and its anachronistic rites. On 5 March 1956 the new recruit was interviewed for membership and, six days later, he was inducted in the presence of his family, friends and Bernadette Allain at the St-Nicolas-des-Champs church in Paris. A black-and-white photograph from the ceremony reveals that his chosen coat of arms resembled a blue monochrome with a border of silver and his personal motto became the heroic, handwritten declaration, 'For Colour! Against line and drawing!'[19] He also added a personal oath, 'Dubbed a knight of the Order of St Sebastian, I espouse the cause of pure colour, which has been invaded by trickery, occupied and oppressed, weakened by line and its manifestation as drawing in art. I espouse the cause of pure colour in order to defend it, to deliver it, and to lead it to triumph in its final glory.'[20]

Around the same time, Marie Raymond had discovered that her husband, Fred, had started consorting with the English painter Ursula Bardsley, news that would lead to a painful separation and eventually a divorce in 1961. After 30 years of marriage the familial netting that Marie and Fred had woven around their son was suddenly coming apart and, once again, he was torn between geographic and affective allegiances. In the summer of 1956 Klein headed to the South of France to visit Tantine and his mother, who had left Fred and retreated to their house in La-Colle-sur-Loup. This 'homecoming' was different from previous ones since Klein both presented himself and was recognized as an artist. In this period, he began to delve into the writings of the nineteenth-century painter Eugène Delacroix as an inspiration for his own ideas on colour. Claiming to be Delacroix's 'disciple', Klein described his project as one revolving around a search for 'sympathetic states, a real or an imaginary landscape, an object, a person, or quite simply a cloud of unknown sensibility through which by chance I suddenly traverse, an ambience . . . It is this "indefinable", this inexpressible moment that I desire to fix on my canvas.'[21] Serving as both a personal diary and an address book, Klein made sure to always have a tape recorder in hand. Such gestures did not go unnoticed by his childhood friends, who remarked the profound change in him. Perhaps the most severe breach occurred with Claude Pascal, who debuted a collection of poems titled *L'Occident est Bleu* (The Occident is Blue), arranged by avant-garde musician Pierre Henry and read by noted actors Michel Vitold and Sylvia Montfort, as a 33 rpm vinyl record. Klein did not attend the record's launch.

Focused on his artistic calling, Klein's primary reason for travelling south was his inclusion, with other emerging artists, in a prestigious show organized by the critic Michel Ragon and the scenographer Jacques Polieri for the first *Festival de l'Art Avant-Garde* (4–21 August 1956). The multidisciplinary event, which presented works by Jean Tinguely, Sam Francis, Serge Poliakoff, Yaacov Agam, Jesús Rafael Soto, Pierre Soulages and Hans Hartung, took place on the roof terrace of Le Corbusier's recently completed collective housing building, L'Unité d'Habitation, in Marseilles. Klein's contribution to the exhibition was a red monochrome similar in size and format to the painting that had been rejected from the Salon des Réalités Nouvelles the previous year. It is possible that he exhibited a comparable painting to create a visible tongue-in-cheek link between his avant-gardiste gesture of refusal vis-à-vis the criteria of the Salon and his willing participation in this self-identified avant-garde event. Against Klein's intention, the red painting had also become a decorative element in Le Corbusier's almost entirely functionalist building. The architect's only compromise to the personal taste of the building's inhabitants was a multicoloured facade and coloured panels within each apartment. Though he wished to release colour from decorative conventions, Klein's work might still have been perceived as an attempt at architectural polychromy in the context of the Unité d'Habitation.

In November 1956 Klein was able to rent a studio at 9 rue Campagne-Première, the bustling artist's enclave in the heart of Montparnasse. With the money he earned teaching judo at the American Center, he was also able to rent a small room at the Hotel Raspail and dine more frequently at La Coupole. On the heels of the group show in Marseilles, Klein was keen to maintain momentum and secure another exhibition as quickly as possible. His first visit was to Iris Clert, a divorcée of Greek origins, who had opened a pioneering gallery sometimes described as 'the smallest gallery of Paris' in Saint-Germain-des-Prés on 2 February 1956.[22] Without an official introduction or an arranged meeting, Klein sauntered into her gallery at 3 rue des Beaux-Arts with an orange monochrome under his arm. Incredulous at his boldness, Clert was taken by Klein's charisma and, by the end of their meeting, she had been convinced to keep the painting for a week and observe how it affected her perceptions. Clert placed the monochrome on a stand and displayed it in her gallery's window, eliciting the mockery of passers-by, neighbours and students at the conservative art school L'Ecole des Beaux Arts. In her autobiography, *Iris-Time*, she observed that her window 'became "the chief attraction" of the Left Bank'.[23] Clert noted the monochrome's immense power to disrupt the status quo, which persuaded her that Klein's work was not without its avant-garde merits. They struck up a friendship that would soon turn into a professional collaboration (and some suspected a romantic liaison).[24] In the meantime an introduction by Pierre Restany brought the Italian gallery owner Guido Le Noci to Klein's studio in November 1956, and, following a tentative meeting, an exhibition was scheduled for the quietest and most innocuous time of the year: the first two weeks of January 1957.

This opportunity to exhibit in Milan propelled Klein into the famous 'blue period', which formally began in 1957 with the aptly titled exhibition *Proposte monochrome/epoca blu* (Monochrome Propositions: Blue Epoch) at the Galleria Apollinaire on the via Brera (2–12 January 1957). In consultation with his mother, Bernadette Allain, Pierre Restany and Iris Clert, who have all taken credit for prompting his decision, Klein eventually eliminated all colours other than blue from his palette. He believed that blue had a unique relation to space. Waxing poetic, he writes,

> Blue has no dimensions. 'It is' beyond dimension while other colors possess it . . . All the colors bring with them associations of concrete, material, tangible ideas, while blue is suggestive of the sea and the sky.[25]

Because of its ubiquity – gracing both sky and sea – Klein considered blue the most universal colour in the spectrum. While this Symbolist evocation seems to refer directly to the nineteenth-century French poet Stéphane Mallarmé, over the years Klein wove a wide web of suggestive images around the colour by absorbing the words of various writers and philosophers, including the Comtesse de Noailles, Paul Eluard, Paul Claudel and Gaston Bachelard. In this expanded realm of resonance, blue was at once 'a flowing liquid', 'an enormous flame', 'a painted vault', 'obscurity become visible' and a space of 'indeterminate reverie'.[26] The colour's dreamlike quality and lack of dimension were especially important for Klein, who was often to quote Gaston Bachelard's mysterious dictum: 'first is *nothing*, then there is a *deep* nothing, then there is a blue *depth*.'[27]

Still using the special solution concocted with the help of Edouard Adam and the company Rhône-Poulenc in 1956, Klein settled on a shade of ultramarine blue that was marketed as number 1311. Though the exact proportions remain secret to this day, a note for the treatment of 700 kg recommends: '1,200 Kg of Rhodopas MA; 2,200 Kg of 95 proof, denatured ethyl alcohol; 0,600 ethyl acetate. Or 4 kg to mix when cold. Never to be heated, danger!'[28] In 1957 these experiments led to a combination of ultramarine pigment and special binder that Klein dubbed International Klein Blue (IKB). This specific colour was Klein's point of departure for the *Epoca Blu* exhibition: an installation that consisted of eleven virtually identical, unframed IKB monochromes, each measuring approximately 30 by 22 inches (78 x 56 cm), with rounded corners and a matte, slightly rippled surface. Each of the uniformly sized panels was attached to a wooden stanchion and hung on brackets that projected it about 6–8 inches (20 cm) in front of the wall. Some were hung at eye level while others were arranged at different heights. Resembling free-floating signposts or billboards, these monochromes asserted the importance of the wall while also protruding into the spectator's physical space and becoming an object of everyday life. The only monochrome that deviated from this analogous set was a red one that hung in Le Noci's private office. It was initially purchased by the important Milanese collector Giuseppe Panza di Biumo, but was returned almost immediately when he changed his mind.[29] Klein's claim that all the paintings were sold was entirely fabricated. In the end only three blue monochromes found a home: they went to the artist Lucio Fontana, the businessman Peppino Palazzoli and Italo Magliano, the former tailor to Benito Mussolini who had reinvented himself as a collector of contemporary art. The young artist Piero

Manzoni did not buy a painting but was riveted by what he saw. Five years Klein's junior, Manzoni absorbed Klein's monochromatic lessons and in 1957 began his series of 'achromes' – completely white canvases made of gesso imbued with glue and liquid kaolin.

The *Epoca Blu* exhibition remains pivotal, both in Klein's lifetime and after, and its analysis could occupy an entire chapter. Whether factual or just a retrospective claim, one of the primary reasons for its importance hinges on Klein's alleged sale of each monochrome at a different price. In his famous retelling of the event Klein insisted that each of his 'blue propositions, all similar in appearance, were perceived by the public as clearly distinct from each other'. What captivated each 'buyer' was the unique 'essence' and 'atmosphere' of each monochrome, a 'pictorial quality' that had nothing to do with the work's 'material' or 'physical' characteristics. This provocative attack on painting's objective limits was intensified by the artist's claim that the poetic singularity of each work went hand in hand with a variable exchange value that he alone determined (around 25,000 lira). In Klein's account, the fact that buyers were willing to pay different prices for identical monochromes meant that each spectator 'entered a state of instant contemplation into the world of blue', an experience that Klein attributed to the monochrome's diffusion of 'pictorial sensibility'.[30] As strange as Klein's declarations may sound today, it appears that he earnestly believed that the monochromes of the *Epoca Blu* period agitated the spectators by provoking an affective transfiguration and initiating a new type of perceptive and sensorial experience.

From our contemporary perspective, his words and actions are important because they expanded the possibility of what painting might be. Paving the way for what the art historian Rosalind Krauss has termed the 'post-medium condition', Klein moved away from a reductive definition of the 'medium' as a physical support with a unique essence and elided it with external factors that activated it conceptually in new ways.[31] The modernist illusion of self-contained artistic autonomy was shattered by the intertwining of the monochrome with a number of contingent conditions and operations. These included a discursive lattice spun by Klein and Restany, the architectural specificities of the gallery, the physiological particularities of the spectator's body and a market economy. Was the exhibition an early instance of performance art, in which the 'liveness' and unrepeatable 'immediacy' of the event trumped the supposedly unchanging, enclosed notion of painting? Was it an instance of proto-conceptual art, in which the idea is the art and the fabrication of an actual object is strictly optional? Klein's activation of the *Epoca Blu* monochromes as triggers that function beyond their physical limits point in all of these directions.

What nags critics most, perhaps, is the way that Klein positioned himself in relation to the historical avant-garde while seeming to mock their utopian ideals. Of course, Restany helped Klein in this endeavour by penning a rousing text that positioned Klein as a social agitator equal to the likes of Piet Mondrian and Kasimir Malevich. 'These monochrome propositions', he declared, 'require of you readers that parcel of responsibility that makes revolutions and defeats tyrants. Modern citizens, with dull-witted intellectual inheritance, intoxicated with the object, with form and with rhythm, how are you going to react to this phenomenon of pure contemplation?'[32] Restany's fighting words and Klein's blue worlds appealed to the prominent Italian writer Dino Buzzati, whose article in the *Corriere d'Informazione*, aptly titled 'Blu, Blu, Blu', brought droves to Le Noci's gallery. Buzzatti was equally attentive to the gallery's reputation as the works' formal aspect. 'I've been told that this place is the lair of the most outrageous avant-garde, that it's the most polemical space in Italy, which hosts live events, madmen, anarchists, revolutionaries, terrorists, and the fanatics of the extreme avant-garde.'[33] Buzzati also noted that it is impossible to differentiate between the blue monochromes or detect the distinct emotional states in which they were painted.

As for the public's reaction, Buzzatti observed the majority's disdain for Klein's mockery of good taste, the minority's appreciation for the exhibition's spiritual dimension and the 'minority of the minority's' understanding of its radicality.[34] Others, like Marco Valsecchi, admonished Restany for equating Klein's monochromes with radical precedents like Mondrian and Malevich. More recently art historians such as Thierry de Duve have argued that unlike the monochromes of the historical avant-garde, which were made in the revolutionary aim of abolishing capitalism, Klein fetishized colour as a unique commodity that could not be separated from a burgeoning capitalist market.[35] With almost all trace of the artist's hand suppressed by the use of the common paint roller, Klein's monochromes announced themselves as mass-produced commodities sold according to the laws of supply and demand. Klein, the self-professed proprietor of colour, tried to evade or minimize this fact by framing his blue propositions as sites of 'pictorial sensibility', a turn of phrase that sounds faintly like New Age Mysticism.[36] This fantastic exultation was aided by Restany's verdict that the colour blue is 'disengaged from all functional justification'.[37] In short, Klein simultaneously occupied two postures that seem incommensurable for an avant-garde artist: on the one hand, reminding us of Karl Marx's definition of the commodity, he collapsed the aesthetic with the political-economic field and elided the quality of each painting with a quantitative exchange value. On the other, he claimed to transgress the laws of the market by discursively endowing each blue monochrome with a unique qualitative potency. The sceptical might very well claim that this evocation of the immaterial was only a reference to a fetishized aura emitted by the commodity object, one that fulfilled the bourgeois public's longing for an authentic experience of life. There is no doubt that his paradoxical strategy of trans-forming painting into a commodity object and enfolding it within a discourse of spirituality was an extremely significant act. Like it or not, he created an expanded field for what it meant to be an avant-garde artist, nurtured by the paradoxical desires of advanced capitalism in mid-twentieth-century France. For an artist who barely suffered the indignation of labouring in obscurity, 1957 was a breakthrough year.

To celebrate his 'triumph' in Milan, Aunt Rose presented her nephew with a three-piece suit tailored especially for him. After spending a week in Nice, Klein returned to Paris in mid-January and unveiled his bright red velvet waistcoat, complemented by a black jacket and trousers, at the fete for St Sebastian's feast day on 20 January.

6

Charlatan, 1957–8

What is sensibility? It is what exists beyond our being yet belongs
to us always. Life itself does not belong to us. It is with our own
sensibility that we can purchase life. Sensibility is the currency
of the universe, of space, of Nature. It allows us to purchase life
in the first material state.[1]

Following the exhibition at the Galleria Apollinaire, Klein's name
circulated widely in avant-garde circles, most notably in Italy and
Germany. With this instantaneous publicity, he realized that riling
both the art establishment and the bourgeois public only reinforced
his notoriety and, from this moment on, each of his actions was
geared toward goading and vexing these two constituencies.
Predating Joseph Beuys' and Andy Warhol's exploits, Klein was
clever enough to orchestrate a double feat. He expertly courted,
nurtured and assumed the personas assigned to the artist by *both* the
defenders and the detractors of the avant-garde: the elite and mass
public. He seamlessly occupied the role of the avant-garde artist,
who could only be understood by a few initiated 'insiders', and that
of the charlatan, accused of deceiving or pulling a 'hoax' on the
mass public. By revealing that these two aspects were equal parts
of paradoxical persona, Klein dismantled the avant-garde artist's
supposed moral authority and, by extension, the charlatan's
alleged depravity. But Klein went a step further and expanded the
critique of this false artistic dichotomy to imagine a different kind

of public. In the exhibitions *Yves Klein: Proposition Monochrome* (Monochrome Proposition) and *Le Vide* (The Void), Klein exposed the interconnectivity between two publics that were theoretically differentiated by taste, education and politics and suggested that they were linked by a universal access to a field of affects that had not yet been dissected or properly regimented, or, in his words, 'sensibility'.

In a witty snub to the official Salon, usually held in the month of May, Iris Clert opened an exhibition titled *The April Micro-Salon* at her tiny gallery on 12 April 1957. The 23 participating artists, including Marie Raymond, Fred Klein and Yves Klein, were asked to contribute small works. This family affair was a symbolic rite of passage in which Klein was finally on a par with his parents, but it was soon eclipsed by bigger and better things. In a brief three-month period between May and July 1957, Klein had solo exhibitions in Paris, Düsseldorf and London. Perhaps the most important was the double manifestation *Yves Klein: Proposition Monochrome*, which took place almost concurrently at the Galerie Iris Clert (12–25 May 1957) on the Left Bank and the Galerie Colette Allendy (14–23 May 1957) on the Right Bank. Targeting both the intelligentsia and bourgeoisie, the two events and their respective *vernissages* were publicized by a single postcard that was itself a work of art. Klein covered one side of the card in his trademark blue while, on the obverse, Restany made vast claims: 'The mono-chrome propositions of Yves KLEIN secure the sculptural destiny of pure pigment today. This grand history of the blue period will be retraced simultaneously on the walls of Colette Allendy and Iris Clert.'[2] Klein designed a blue perforated stamp, approved and validated by the post office (with extra monetary incentive), and affixed it to each card. The dimensions of this stamp were very close to the size of a real stamp, which in turn approximated the proportions of many of Klein's paintings, which fluctuate between about 5:3.5 and 5:4.[3]

Self-promotion was always on Klein's mind. But this was more than a marketing ploy: the stamp was a 'mini manifesto' that made visible the structural operations of Klein's art practice. His witty infiltration of the state postal system turned his works into a rare collector's item as well as a democratic medium for communication. Beginning with the monochromes of the *Epoca Blu* exhibition, all of Klein's work emerged from a system of equivalence, by which art objects could not be separated from a market economy and its bureaucratic institutions. He demonstrated the importance of mass media channels not only for broadcasting an already composed and completed message but for contributing to the very formation of speech acts through a medium's specific format and technology. His International Klein Blue stamp resonated with two very common stamps issued between 1945 and 1959, which bore the image of Marianne, the symbol for the French Republic.[4] Klein surely knew that the 1957 version was ultramarine blue. In this very small gesture of citation Klein situated the monochrome at the cusp between the absurd and the official and tested the threshold between aesthetic proposition and political act. Again and again his modus operandi was to perturb the public's expectations of where the boundaries between art and life began and ended. He executed this in a number of steps: first, he obliged viewers to question whether the objects they encountered in art institutions and public spaces were 'real'. Second, and much more challenging, he provoked viewers to critically consider the collective conventions that led them to make this decision. Third, he incited viewers to alter these precepts through an art practice that imagined new forms of communicative structures.

Since Clert's store front space measured a mere 20 square metres, Klein decided to exhibit a small selection of blue monochromes and a single, blue sponge sculpture. Since the late 1940s the French artist Jean Dubuffet had been introducing various textural elements into his paintings, so Klein was not alone in this practice. Yet according to Edouard Adam, Klein's 'discovery' of natural sponges as an artistic medium was inspired by seeing them displayed in his shop window in 1956.[5] Klein became enamoured with the form and texture of the 'impregnated' sponge, though he was not totally pleased with its irregular qualities.[6] Hearkening to Dubuffet's defence of Art Brut and its 'savage values', Klein described sponges as 'savage, living material' that would be transformed into unique art objects and, more poetically, a 'portrait' of the 'reader' of his monochromes.[7] Viewers of his blue paintings, he said, would be saturated 'in sensibility, just as the sponges' and would undergo a cognitive transformation through this artistic encounter.[8] At Clert's Klein accompanied the artworks by a looped soundtrack of his one-note musical piece known as the *Monotone Symphony*. This composition was recorded by Pierre Henry, a classically trained pianist and percussionist who was at the forefront of France's concrete music movement. Formed in 1951 by Henry, Pierre Schaeffer and Jacques Poullin, this group of musicians captured sounds from non-musical sources (dogs barking, footsteps, trains chugging along tracks) and manipulated them electronically to create novel pieces. By drawing on Pierre Henry to compose the *Monotone Symphony*, Klein benefitted from the former's avant-garde credentials to solidify his own nascent status.

Using common materials was not new in the annals of avant-gardism. Found and readymade objects were the very basis of Marcel Duchamp's and the Surrealists' redefinition of the category of art in the early and mid-twentieth century. It was Klein's addition of promotional theatrical tactics that many found distasteful. Not everyone shared Iris Clert's conviction that releasing 1,001 blue helium balloons into the sky of Saint-Germain on opening night, in sight of the venerable Café Deux Magots, was a brilliant way to '[attract] Parisians' attention to the young unknown artist'.[9] Even if Klein named this spectacle his 'first aero-static sculpture', the aggrieved critic Claude Rivière condemned the stunt as 'shameful!

It's commercial publicity!'[10] This was also a turning point in Klein's relationship with Guy Debord, a founding member of the Situationist International. In the early to mid-1950s their complicity was such that Klein invited Debord to contribute a text for this double exhibition; yet Debord refused, probably on account of Klein's adherence to Rosicrucianism and affiliation to the Order of St Sebastian. For Debord, who was closer to the writings of Karl Marx than Max Heindel, these mystical organizations reeked of reactionary rather than progressive tendencies, rendering Klein a dubious character.[11] Though Debord visited Klein's exhibition at the Galerie Colette Allendy, he recoiled from Klein's penchant for spectacle – 'a social relationship between people that is mediated by images' – which was an integral part of his 'charlatan' persona.[12]

More susceptible to Klein's commercial tactics, Mr Stanley Marcus from Dallas, Texas, one of the two American collectors who purchased a monochrome from Iris Clert, described the work's effect in a telling letter: 'My Yves Klein has proved to be one of the most sensational purchases I have ever made. It has brought great laughter and fun whenever I show it. I will be sending you lots of customers this summer.'[13] In this case, Klein's avant-gardism was sanctioned by a classic response from 'the common man'. Marcus's baffled amusement was a sure-fire way to compensate for an inability to understand Klein's work. More extreme than Debord and Marcus was the rejoinder of an anonymous passer-by who wrote 'mort aux vaches' on the gallery's window.[14] This slur dates to the Franco-Prussian war of the 1870 when German soldiers stationed in Paris had the word 'WACHE' inscribed on their watch posts. Some twenty years later, in the 1890s, the French anarchists adopted it as their cry against all forms of government. It is difficult to decide whether this particular graffiti denounced Klein as representing the powerful establishment or if it embraced him as an intransigent brother in arms. Klein seemed to consider it a threat because he invited his *judoka* friends to work as security guards at the opening.

He used similarly spectacular strategies at the opening of his exhibition at the Galerie Colette Allendy. On 14 May 1957, as night was falling, Klein attached sixteen Bengal flares to a blue monochrome painting placed on an easel and lit them all simultaneously for one minute. This was an important if rather literal demonstration that his paintings were 'the ashes' of his art, which only lived as a trace in the viewer's memory. Such pyrotechnics, steeped in spiritual discourse, did not endear Klein to the doyenne of Geometric Abstraction, Denise René, for whom abstraction was a politically engaged visual form whose burning was an unforgivable sacrilege.[15] Meanwhile, inside the gallery, Klein deconstructed the blue monochrome into an array of eclectic, inventive objects. The walls were covered with two large *Blue Tapestries*, one hung vertically and the other horizontally. Klein noted that, 'at one meter away, it is a simple, rich fabric. At three meters it is a tapestry. At eight meters, it is a painting in the total pictorial sense.'[16] There were also two rows of vertically arranged cube-shaped reliefs, *Blue Reliefs*, resembling building blocks or the 'specific-objects' that the American minimalist Donald Judd would make a decade later. A circular form with a granular surface, *Blue Disk*, hung in the middle of the gallery wall and appeared like a planetary element in space. The ceiling emanated *Blue Rain*, an assemblage of thin wooden extensions that seemed to glide in space; part of the floor was covered by grains of *Pure Pigment*, laid down like a carpet in a rectangular expanse with no fixative and brushed with a rake to create coiling patterns. Two Japanese-inspired *Folding Screens*, one placed on a table and the other on the bed of blue pigment, could be observed from different angles. *Blue Trap for Lines* consisted of a flat surface with spiny blue, jutting outcrops. And a *Blue Obelisk*, of which we have no documentation, was raised off its base with a metal rod so that it seemed to levitate.

The saturation of space with hybrid objects, each appealing differently to the eye of the spectator, demanding a bodily inter-action and altering the value of space by its architectonic structure, suggests that Klein's focus was the effect of distance. To deconstruct the traditional framework for the perception of reality, he tried to gradually abolish the artificially constructed convention of distance – or depth – between spectator and object. After seeing this exhibition, Louis-Paul Favre, the critic at the newspaper *Combat*, positively noted that Klein sought 'a form that is able to *touch* each person in the public realm'.[17] Much less affirmative, other critics characterized Klein as 'a man who likes to deceive himself' and who is '[mocking] the world . . . to try to make us believe in innovation at any price'.[18] His monochromes were suspected of being 'a spiritual joke', and even worse, a 'painting of madness . . . the folly of painting . . . an inflation of nonsense!'[19] An astute comment in the newspaper *Le Monde* noted, 'At last, it would be amusing, once and for all, to fix the limits beyond which avant-garde painting would not be able to go.'[20] The implication is that there is a very thin line between being an avant-garde artist and a charlatan.

One can only imagine how these critics would have reacted had they seen the most radical part of the exhibition. Klein designed *Surfaces and Blocks of Invisible Pictorial Sensibility* for the second floor of Allendy's gallery and only invited his intimate circle to attend. Painted completely white and left totally empty, this space was once Dr René Allendy's consultation room, in which he had treated the likes of Anaïs Nin and Antonin Artaud. Turned into an artwork, it was a space to bask in the 'immaterial ambience' of painting's sensibility.[21] When one considers the centrality of paint-ing in post-war France – both abstract and figurative – as a means of representing the world, Klein's act becomes truly exhilarating. Circa 1957, no other French artist strove to structurally alter painting's possibilities in such radical ways. To teach the public how to interact with a space that aimed to eliminate all 'supports' and present pure ambience, Klein made a short 16 mm colour film documenting the installation. It shows him looking intently at the blank walls from different angles. The camera pans to a piece of wood placed on a small radiator, which trembles vigorously for no apparent reason. Klein stops the agitation with his hand. In this staged pedagogical performance the artist seems to be alerting the spectator to 'ghosts' in the room.[22] We can speculate that Klein was playfully revealing the powerful traces that hindered his search for purity or, alternatively, that he was associating himself with the practices of earlier avant-gardists such as Nin and Artaud who were also grappling with the body's relation to art making.

In quick succession Klein exhibited his monochromes in Düsseldorf, at the inauguration of the Alfred Schmela Gallery (31 May–23 June 1957), and in London at Gallery One (24 June– 13 July 1957). He was absolutely ecstatic, considering his show in Germany 'a triumph'; gloating at the 'formidable impact' of the two exhibitions in Paris; and asserting that his name is 'as presently well known as that of Picasso!' The only thing left, he wrote to Aunt Rose, was to 'conquer the United States'.[23] With this rapid ascent, Klein started to drift apart from Bernadette Allain. In early July 1957, on a trip to Nice, he met the astonishingly beautiful Rotraut Uecker, who he dubbed 'Trot Trot'. The younger sister of the German artist and founder of the Zero Group Günther Uecker, she was only nineteen years old, ten years Klein's junior, and did not then have a good command of French. Born in Rerik, a small town on the Baltic Sea, she had left East Germany in 1956 to pursue a life in the arts and joined her brother in Düsseldorf (where she had seen Klein's exhibition at the Galerie Schmela) before coming to Nice in the summer of 1957 and taking up the post of au pair for Arman's three children. According to Rotraut, her meeting with Klein was a case of love at first sight.[24] He courted her with verve and for a month they spent most days and nights together. Rotraut recalls that at the end of that summer he sadly announced that they would not see each other again.[25] He was obviously mistaken; but in late 1957 Klein was intently focused on his work and dreaming of the fame it would bring him.

Compared with the achievements of the Blue Period, *Surfaces and Blocks of Invisible Pictorial Sensibility* was a 'minor' work. Nevertheless, it was a crucial conceptual catalyst that helped Klein shift from the language of painting to a preoccupation with space. Arguably the most momentous result of this line of investigation was *The Void*, which opened at the Galerie Iris Clert on 28 April 1958, the night of Klein's thirtieth birthday. His aspiration was to

> create, to establish, and to impress upon the viewing public a sensuous pictorial state within the confines of an art gallery; in other words, the creation of an environment, of a real pictorial climate, therefore one that is invisible. This invisible pictorial state within the space of the gallery must literally become what until now has been given as the best general definition of painting: 'radiance.'
>
> For the creative act to succeed, the immaterialization of the invisible and intangible canvas must act upon the sensuous vehicles or bodies of gallery visitors with much more efficiency than ordinary, physical representational paintings . . . These intermediaries are now no longer needed: one is literally impregnated with the pictorial sensibility, refined and stabilized beforehand by the painter in a given space. It is direct and immediate perception and assimilation without other effects, without gadgets or hoaxes.[26]

The few surviving black-and-white photographs show a small, empty room with an unfilled vitrine in one corner and a draped doorway in the other. There are neither people nor art objects in the space, only a perfect stillness illuminated by a solitary neon light. The gallery seems totally abandoned and far from being an art manifestation of any consequence. If we are to believe Klein's breathless retelling, retrospectively written in the present tense, *The Void* was one of the most well-attended art events of 1958. Klein claimed that 3,000 people congested the rue de Seine on the night of the exhibition's inauguration and that several hundred people attended each day until it closed on 12 May 1958.[27] Klein most likely exaggerated the numbers, but the fact that Iris Clert extended the show for another week suggests that the turnout was unusually large. Even the writer Albert Camus paid his respects, giving Klein a scrap of paper (embossed with the *Nouvelle Revue Française*'s insignia) with the phrase 'Avec Le Vide, Les Pleins Pouvoir' (With The Void, Full Powers).

To expand his practice beyond the confines of the canvas, Klein carefully planned and executed a series of interrelated episodes and occurrences in the public sphere. Advertisements were placed in the Parisian journals *Arts* and *Combat* and posters were hung throughout Saint-Germain-des-Prés. An invitation with a text by Restany inscribed in blue ink on a white card was sent, purportedly to 3,500 people, with Klein's blue stamp. It exhorted the public to bring their 'affective presence' to a 'manifestation of perceptive synthesis', which testified to the artist's 'pictorial quest for ecstatic and immediately communicable emotion'.[28] Eliding affect with money, Klein cheekily warned that without this card visitors would have to pay an admission price of 1,500 old francs. The upshot was that Klein imposed a penalty for not being a card-carrying member of his private 'club'. Once again Klein hired his *judoka* friends as security guards, claiming that he 'anticipated acts of vandalism'.[29] He also stationed Republican Guards, in full regalia, at the entrance to the gallery to endow the exhibition with an 'official character'.[30] Blue cocktails were concocted by the barman at La Coupole using gin, Cointreau and methylene blue and served in a small adjoining corridor as the hordes waited to enter the gallery. This particular recipe was intentionally designed to tint the drinker's urine deep blue, thus 'marking' or 'branding' the public as Klein's artworks, and distributing them pell-mell throughout the city of Paris. The final touch of this elaborate spectacle was Klein's plan to use a helicopter to drop a blue fabric on top of the obelisk at the Place de la Concorde. When this became too expensive to execute, he decided to illuminate the obelisk in blue light. Regrettably, the police department denied permission for this stunt at the last minute, citing it as being 'too personal in character and [attracting] too much publicity'.[31]

Klein used a symbolic colour scheme of blue and white to organize the public's initiation into *The Void*. He sealed off the main entrance of the gallery and painted its front window blue. The doorway that adjoined the gallery, normally an entrance for the inhabitants of the building, was swathed with flamboyant blue drapery to clearly direct the visitors through it. Past this doorway, a small passageway – approximately 32 square metres – led to the main exhibition space. A blue curtain on the passageway's left wall shielded the doorway into this room while a white curtain hung on its other side. Through it was the empty gallery space whose walls Klein claims to have spent the previous 48 hours whitewashing in seclusion. His friends Jean-Pierre Mirouze, Bernadette Allain and Charles Le Moing all recall that they helped in the endeavour.[32] Using a ripolin enamel roller, they covered the walls with several coats of pure white lithopane pigment blended with Klein's special varnish of alcohol, acetone and vinyl resin. Devoid of all traditional art objects, the room had only an empty vitrine stationed in its left corner and a small table in the store-front window. Both objects were painted white 'to receive the pictorial climate of sensibility of dematerialized blue'.[33] Only the floors were carpeted in light grey and a sole fluorescent light illuminated the room.

Can we cast our minds back to 1958 and imagine this strange emptiness filled with a curious crowd of people who came in search of an authentic aesthetic and social experience? How would the various constituencies of the public – artists, critics and passers-by – have understood this seminal art event? There have been various interpretations in the intervening years, each privileging a different aspect of the manifestation. Like many avant-garde works of the twentieth century, *The Void* was for the most part misunderstood and maligned at the moment of its appearance. The more positive reviews expressed shock and pleasure at the newness of the event: 'The taste of the unusual and even the extravagant is worth more than the love of the beaten track: it excites the spirit', wrote Jean Grenier in *Preuves*.[34] The critic for *Combat* noted that 'Yves Klein . . . tries here to tackle the synthesis of light itself and to do so without intellectualism and without witticism. It is thus not a joke but the recognition of a power, of a magic of colour.'[35] The majority of the French press could not overcome their suspicion of Klein's charlatanism and claimed the work was a hoax or joke played on an unsuspecting audience. 'It's too much! Are they mocking us? Thus do, do, do the marionettes of Saint-German-des-Prés', heralded *Figaro*, while *Aux Ecoutes* condemned Klein for a 'reign of the sensible' which was merely 'a white wall like the one in a freshly lime-washed cowshed'.[36] 'Exhibition of white' claimed *La Croix*, while *Arts* remarked that 'Yves Klein gets rid of Iris Clert's worry of hanging paintings in her gallery.'[37] 'Immediately commercial emotion', observed the more incisive *L'Echo Liberté*.[38]

More recently, scholars have begun to articulate *The Void*'s complexity in different terms. The astute French art historian Denys Riout has situated *The Void* as the last step in an artistic progression that began with Klein's blue monochromes of 1957. Following Klein's own claims, he emphasizes the way in which this installation enacted the liberation of 'pictorial sensibility' from the material support of the monochrome.[39] Taking the argument a step further, Benjamin H. D. Buchloh has contended that *The Void* enacted the 'spatialization of painterly reductivism', an avant-garde strategy previously performed by El Lissitzky in the 1920s that 'shifts the scale of the framing device: From the level of easel paintings . . . to the level of architecture itself.'[40] Not only did Klein transform the gallery space as a 'zone of heightened pictorial, proto-mystical sensibility',[41] as Riout suggests, but this same gallery space became the artwork itself. There are numerous artistic and political implications to this shift: Klein was among a generation of artists whose interest in dismantling the autonomy of art led to the critique of the art institution as an ideological space. The point was to bare the agendas and interests of galleries and museums and to suggest that politics permeated even the most ostensibly neutral containers. It must be remembered that Klein was operating in a highly charged moment in French politics, at the height of the Algerian War, between the fall of the Fourth Republic on 15 April 1958 and the establishment of the Fifth Republic on 1 June 1958. His parodic use of Republican Guards and his revoked effort to illuminate the obelisk might have been understood in the context of Charles de Gaulle's return to power and the nervousness about what kind of government he would form. Paradoxically, while the Parisian masses thronged to *The Void*, the space was a conceptual performance of the existing uncertainty and anxiety in the public sphere.

By Klein's own admission he was on a mission to connect his art to political ends. Here, too, his seemingly irreconcilable objectives seem to waver between regressive and progressive tendencies, and may leave many sceptical about his standing as an avant-garde artist. In an unpublished document, he asserted, 'I realize that to continue and to evolve in my monochromatic and pneumatic pictorial work (in the sense of abstract sensibility), I find myself obliged to take power in France.'[42] To this megalomaniacal end, he sketched the outlines of a provisory government of rehabilitation, one that would emerge from the expansion of painting into space.

Klein's statement, pronounced at *La Coupole* immediately after the vernissage of *The Void*, is so multi-layered and poignant that it is worth quoting in its entirety. In order to 'turn France into an immediate and radiant vision', Klein proposed

> An order of chivalry where artists, religious and scientific men, will give France back its rightful color, blue or white, perhaps even amaranth, and will efface the miasmas of a horrible France, green, red, and gray, of a leprous France; This government will give back to its soldiers the ornate uniforms of Napoleon III and the lead soldiers of our child- hood and it will purify us, like holy water cleanses the devil from those to whom we can say, with Cicero: '*Quousque tandem Catilina abutere patientia nostra*' (Until when, Catilina, will you abuse our patience?). Our pure and scandalous government will eliminate the false fellows, the Françoise Sagans, the liars, the Genets, the Georges Duhamels, the Einsteins, the Roosevelts, the Pandit Nehrus, the rats and the garbage cans, etc., etc. May it be said and done.[43]

This bizarre and hermetic invective against contemporary figures in the arts, letters, sciences and politics cannot easily be penetrated. What Sagan has in common with Nehru, or Genet with Roosevelt, in Klein's mind, is virtually impossible to determine. What emerges from this diatribe, however, is Klein's religious and royalist attitude and his extreme concern for the salubrious ('pure') state of the nation. This fear may well be connected to the four years of German Occupation, which incited national purges in the war's immediate aftermath, and to the ongoing de-colonization of Algeria, which went hand in hand with an intensified focus on domestic order.[44] Klein's personal discourse, symptomatic of a right-wing national discourse, did not go unnoticed. Only eight months following this 'revolutionary' speech, Guy Debord would affirm, not surprisingly, that Klein was at the head of the 'fascist wave that progresses in France'.[45]

Following the disintegration and discrediting of the available pre-war models and the absence of a new public order, Klein provided an original fashioning of the problem of the absence of a coherent, sustainable public. With absence as the starting point, what kind of public did Klein envision for France? Though he may have believed he was releasing sensibility from the object and diffusing it as a sort of ambience within space, *The Void* appears to be a spatial environment in which the spectator's experience of their own affect (that is, 'presence' or 'sensibility') became the aesthetic event. Extrapolated into the socio-political sphere, it could feasibly create the basis for a democratic political arrangement of people removed from a strict national affiliation. The common binder between individuals would be universal 'life force' freed from an affinity to a country or nation state. This utopian idea was unfortunately couched in a language of extreme violence, which is what made Klein appear as both an avant-garde artist and a charlatan.

Klein's calling card was precisely this paradoxical duality, which never collapses into an easy resolution. Exacerbating the two fundamental personas that many wished to maintain as far apart as possible, he simultaneously occupied the position of an avant-garde artist (a democratically inclined Republican) and a charlatan (a suspicious reactionary). The meanings of these positions were connected to artistic and historical structures and discourses. It would not be long before he would cross the border into West Germany and travel across the Atlantic to the United States to continue disrupting the epistemological presuppositions upon which these identities were determined.

7

Collaborator, 1957–61

Artists who are unable to collaborate work with the gut,
the plexus, the intestines! Artists who collaborate work with
their hearts and their minds![1]

Klein's debut at the Alfred Schmela gallery in Düsseldorf
(31 May–23 June 1957) was the beginning of a fruitful relationship
with the German artistic scene, which was more open than the
French one to radical experimentation. His exhibition of monochromes brought him into contact with contemporaries such as
Heinz Mack, Otto Piene and Günther Uecker, the founders of
the Zero Group. He also solidified ties with the sculptor Norbert
Kricke and the architect Werner Ruhnau, whom he had recently
met in Paris on the occasion of Kricke's exhibition at the Galerie
Iris Clert in March 1957. Through these acquaintances, Klein was
invited to participate in collaborative projects that necessitated the
cultivation of a new identity. Over a period of four years, between
1957 and 1961, he had ample opportunity to develop and tweak the
persona of the 'collaborator' according to the specific circumstances
of each venture.

In some cases Klein contributed directly to the group enterprise
while in others he imagined new collective dynamics on a more
abstract level. Klein mined the tension between 'collective' and
'collaborator' at significant occasions such as the international
competition to decorate the interior of the Gelsenkirchen

Musiktheater (1957–9), the *Air Architecture* project, a socially
conscious proposal for an architecture that would employ the
energy of air, water and fire as basic construction materials
(1957–62), the exhibition *Yves Klein et Jean Tinguely, Vitesse
pure et stabilité monochrome* at Galerie Iris Clert (1958), and the
constitution of the movement known as Nouveau Réalisme (1960).
In these endeavours he tackled the questions of how to mediate
between the singular identity of the artist and a shared aesthetic
vision of a group, and how to reconcile individual agency while
fostering communal relations.

The Gelsenkirchen project had been long in the making before
Klein became involved and it remains one of the least studied
aspects of his practice. Bordering Essen in the Ruhr region, the
city of Gelsenkirchen was at the centre of Germany's coal mining,
machine manufacture and glass production industries. Like many
other cities in the Ruhr during the 1950s, it underwent massive
reconstruction after its urban complex was destroyed by bombings
and ground attacks in the Second World War. The Münster-based
architectural team of H. Deilmann, M. C. von Hausen, Ortwin
Rave and Werner Ruhnau won the official competition to design
a new music theatre in September 1954 and the foundation stone
was laid in June 1956. After their fortuitous meetings in Paris and
Düsseldorf, Ruhnau invited Klein and Kricke to act as principal
members of the artistic team before announcing the competition
for the decoration of the theatre on 31 May 1957. By the end of the
competition in June 1957, the international group included Robert
Adams, an English sculptor living in London, and Paul Dierkes,
a German sculptor living in West Berlin. Jean Tinguely, the Swiss
sculptor-*bricoleur* and on-site German translator for Klein, joined
the group in November 1958.[2]

Klein was charged with designing works for the theatre's main
lobby and its cloakroom. He was elated to undertake his first major
public commission and, with Bernadette Allain in tow, drove his

new Citroën 2 cv across the border. He could not know that in the tense period of Franco-German political rapprochement, the city's administration was not too pleased about the choice of a French artist and that he would face many hurdles in getting his designs and budget ratified. It probably did not help that Klein could not speak German, which led to occasional conflicts with Werner Ruhnau and a growing paranoia that he was being mocked. As time went on, Jean Tinguely's participation as a full member of the artistic team meant that he could no longer act as Klein's personal translator. After one week at the construction site Bernadette left Gelsenkirchen for Paris and Klein beckoned his new love interest, Rotraut Uecker, to join him. For almost the entire duration of the project, 'Trot' worked side by side with Klein as his assistant and eventually eclipsed Bernadette as his romantic companion. She only departed from Gelsenkirchen in May 1959 after an accident where she almost fell off some scaffolding. Unlike other members of the team, she was uninsured, so Klein sent her to Paris, with the keys to his apartment and the instruction to learn French. From this moment she became his live-in companion and eventually his wife. Despite these emotional, financial and linguistic challenges, Klein produced six huge works for the theatre: two large blue monochromes with ingrained ripple effects (7 x 20 metres) for the eastern and western side walls of the main lobby and four blue sponge reliefs, two placed along the rear wall of the main lobby (5 x 10 metres) and two situated above the lower level cloakroom (3 x 9 metres). Upon its inauguration on 15 December 1959, the *Deutsche Bauzeitung*, a German architectural journal, lauded the Neues Theater im Revier, as it was officially called, as having 'no equivalent'.[3]

Klein's extensive correspondence with Ruhnau suggests a mutual interest in Gelsenkirchen as a model for Franco-German reconciliation within the contemporaneous construction of the European Community. Writing in French, Klein hailed Gelsenkirchen the 'merveilleuse situation Européene' (the marvellous European Situation),[4] and proclaimed 'vive le théâtre de Gelsenkirchen, vive Ruhnau et la situation Européene' (long live Gelsenkirchen, long live Ruhnau and the European Situation).[5] Ruhnau responded in German, 'Viele Grüsse und es lebe die europäische Situation' (all best and long live the European Situation) and 'Paris soll noch viel mehr von der "Europäischen Situation" traumen' (Paris will only dream of the European Situation from now on).[6] In these statements, Klein and Ruhnau positioned the theatre as an ambitious yet unresolved political project, one that negotiated the complex representations of the newly emerging construct of a united Europe as a geographic, economic, sociopolitical and cultural entity. Klein's treatment of the ambiguous European ideal was through an 'aesthetics of collaboration', which would mediate between the particular ego of each artist and the shared achievement of the artwork. His most lucid presentation of the subject occurred at the opening of Jean Tinguely's exhibition in Düsseldorf in January 1959, while both artists were actively working at Gelsenkirchen.

> I would like to put forth to all those who willingly hear me: COLLABORATION! But pay attention to the etymology of the word. To collaborate means precisely to work together on the same project. The project upon which I propose collaboration is Art itself! The source of inexhaustible LIFE through which as true artists we are liberated from the dreamy and picturesque imagination of the psychological realm, which is the anti-space of the PAST, is found in Art . . . Artists who collaborate work with their hearts and their minds! These art artists who know of the RESPONSIBILITY of being HUMAN vis-à-vis the UNIVERSE![7]

While making no explicit allusions to the Second World War, Klein's emphatic reference to 'responsibility' along with the overt directive to heed collaboration's etymology and free oneself from

the tainted past nevertheless takes on the existential overtones
of the writings of the French philosopher Jean-Paul Sartre, one of
the beacons of the left-wing French intelligentsia. For Sartre and
countless other intellectuals who had lived through the staggering
defeat of France in June 1940 and the extraordinary four years of
the Occupation, it was crucial to understand how 'collaboration'
with the enemy became possible. 'Collaboration' signalled many
nuanced forms of submission and accommodation to the Nazi
occupiers at the level of both state and civil society, and the full
historical and moral stakes, which are the topic of profound
research and debate, cannot be given justice here. Nevertheless,
in order to contextualize Klein's appropriation of such a fraught
term, it is important to note that after France's capitulation, Marshal
Philippe Pétain signed an armistice (22 June 1940) that gave the
Germans control over the north and west of the country, including
Paris, while leaving about two-fifths of France's pre-war territory
unoccupied. A week after meeting with Adolf Hitler at Montoire-
sur-le-Loir on 24 October 1940, Petain addressed the nation on the
radio and announced a policy of 'collaboration' between France and
Germany as a way of safeguarding France's unity and preventing
its population from greater suffering. The Pétain-led Vichy regime,
which succeeded the Third Republic from July 1940 and remained
in place until August 1944, wilfully collaborated with Nazi Germany
by, among other policies, taking measures to denaturalize and hunt
down the country's 'undesirables' – including left-wing activists,
freemasons, communists, gypsies, homosexuals, *métèques* (immi-
grants from Mediterranean countries) and Jews. In fact, without
German involvement in domestic policy, France immediately set
up a commission to review its nationality laws and, between June
1940 and August 1944, 15,000 individuals, mostly Jews, were
stripped of their citizenship.[8] Furthermore, France voluntarily
declared the first Statute on Jews (3 October 1940), which enforced
racial segregation and authorized the internment of foreign Jews

on the sole basis of a prefectoral order (4 October 1940). According to the groundbreaking research of historians Robert Paxton and Michael Marrus, Vichy's ideological solidarity with the Third Reich and its own cultural and economic anti-semitism meant a level of cooperation that greatly facilitated the Final Solution: from a population of approximately 300,000 Jews living in metropolitan France in 1940, 76,000 hapless individuals were deported to concentration and extermination camps and only 2,600 ever returned.[9] Long after the Liberation, once the Vichy regime had been declared null and void, the painful and divisive process of coming to terms with the moral, material and political balance sheet of collaboration between France and Germany continued.

In August 1945 Sartre published *Qu'est-ce qu'un collaborateur?*, a diagnosis of collaboration that did much to fortify the mythic image of the French Resistance and marginalize the occurrence of collaboration by characterizing it as an individual pathology.[10] Much like suicide or criminality, the propensity to collaborate, Sartre argued, is present in every collectivity. When the right social conditions are present, a person or social body (mostly deviants, foreigners and marginal types) is 'occupied' by the abject ideas and interests of others and will act out upon this urge as a kind of 'disassimilation' from the indigenous culture. In this formulation Sartre implied that collaboration was not a widespread condition, but a marginal form of behaviour provoked by foreign (that is, German) influences. The only solution, according to Sartre, is to rebel against and purge this abjection from the social body in a national revolution and restore France to its lost unity.

More than a decade after the war, it is well worth asking if there was any real or symbolic power to Klein's recuperation, recycling and rebranding of the French sentiment of shame and self-recrimination into a morally positive, universally accessible act. The question is especially pertinent since, by the late 1950s, 'collaboration' had transmuted into a bevy of less historically burdened expressions (that is, cooperation, association, integration) to mediate Franco–German relations that climaxed in the signing of the Franco–German Treaty of Friendship and Cooperation between Charles de Gaulle and Konrad Adenauer in 1963.[11] It could not have been happenstance that Klein chose this politically loaded word as the basis for an aesthetic strategy to be delivered by a French artist to a German audience on German soil in the years surrounding the construction of the European Union and its debates about Franco–German rapprochement. The word 'collaboration', while undoubtedly evoking the pre-war utopian aspirations of the Bauhaus and the post-war hopes for national reconciliation, was irretrievably contaminated by its political instrumentalization during the Second World War. According to the art historian Nan Rosenthal, 'Klein's proposal to collaborate in art' was an 'attempt by fiat to efface the collaboration in World War II, that is, as an attempt to turn the ambiguous and inevitably guilt-producing collaboration that Sartre described into something moral . . . His attempt, however, also has the effect of raising the very subject it wished to paint over, or forget, or make disappear into a void of history which never happened.'[12] Indeed, it seems extremely likely that Klein mobilized 'collaboration' precisely because the word could not have been purged of all its historically specific meaning and was thus lodged on both sides of a historical divide. Even as it became a morally laudable process for the benevolent reconstruction of Europe, it also retained its morally repugnant connotations as an act that one could never imagine oneself participating in if one's politics were correct, especially in hindsight, with full knowledge of both the Bauhaus's demise upon Hitler's assumption of power in 1933 and the *épuration* (purge) that gripped France immediately after the war.[13] There's also the question of what 'collaboration' signified in Germany (as opposed to France, where Klein also deployed the word in an official speech).[14]

Within Klein's paradigm, collaboration led to a strange conundrum for a German spectator at Gelsenkirchen, as he or she was both encouraged to collaborate and was potentially humiliated, alienated and, in Sartre's judgment, rendered a 'marginal, maladjusted element' by the thought of doing so. Being in the shoes of a collaborator meant living in a condition of crisis, or, as Klein wrote, those who collaborate 'are paradoxically united and separated at the same time'.[15] To be sure, Klein urges artists to continue speaking in the first person within the framework of collaboration ('Me, I, MY, MINE . . . , etc. and not the hypocritical WE, OUR . . . But that, only after having solemnly signed the pact of COLLABORATION'). This articulation posits collaboration as an internally conflicted, heterogeneous experience of identification and refusal, a form of extreme violence to any notion of subjective or historical unity. If we extend this disjunctive state of collaboration to the political realm as the discursive site for Franco–German renewal, Klein's formulation implies that the shared historical burden of the war had to be at least acknowledged by both nations alike in order to imagine the rehabilitated French and German sovereignty necessary for a European consciousness.

The fiction of a United Europe as a new political entity went hand in hand with the development of a new model of community, a form of 'European Citizenship' before the coining of such a term. At Gelsenkirchen, this concept took the form of a spontaneous living arrangement in an old firehouse (Alte Feuerwache) close to the building site. The 'Bauhütte', as it was christened by Helmuth de Haas, editor of the Essen newspaper *Die Welt*, served as the central organ for the theatre's administrative and planning offices as well as the living and sleeping quarters for the international group of bureaucrats, engineers, architects, artists and construction workers.[16] To ensure that this multicultural social experiment would respect the rights of the individual while sustaining a successful group dynamic, Klein and the other residents formalized a contract with a strict set of rules and regulations. Typed in German, the contract covered everything from laundry, groceries, cleaning, repair, fuel, heat and postage costs to sleeping arrangements, daily schedule, expectations for hygiene and order and penalties for breaking the rules. Within this extremely pragmatic living arrangement Klein and Ruhnau founded an idealistic inner sanctum. They called it the 'Blue Patriots Party' and nominated themselves as its primary leaders. As Ruhnau recalls, 'Yves and I were to be "chiefs" for France and Germany and Anita Ruhnau, Bernadette Allain, Franz Krause, Paul Dierkes, and Charles Wilp, among others, were to be members.'[17] Though there was no hard and fast rule, it seems that the role of 'chief' alternated between Klein and Ruhnau each time they crossed the Franco-German border. As it turns out, Klein drove between Paris and Gelsenkirchen on a regular basis while Ruhnau mostly remained on site to manage the construction of the theatre. As a result, Klein ended up appropriating many of the ideas that emerged from their collaborative union and either claiming them as his own or developing them independently of the architect.

Such is the case with the *Air Architecture* project, which emerged from Klein's visionary pursuit of the immaterial and Ruhnau's knowledge of architectural history and engineering. Both outlandish and prescient, Klein and Ruhnau imagined a new type of structural design made entirely out of natural elements. Together they dreamed of using air, water and fire as the building blocks for what Klein called 'the new Garden of Eden' and Ruhnau baptized 'the city of tomorrow'.[18] Air jets funnelled at extremely high pressure would create floating furniture while fire and water would be the basis for thermal conditioning. Protected by a roof of air, nomadic communities would wander the earth nude in complete leisure and take shelter in different 'microclimates'. As a result of this dematerialized architecture, the collective social fabric would be radically altered. Klein noted that the 'psychological family environment' and its 'primitive patriarchal structure' would be destroyed.[19] The 'conception of intimacy' would have to be fundamentally rethought since the community would be 'free, individualistic, and impersonal'.[20] These ideas emerged from a close intellectual and personal partnership and in tandem with other visionary concepts of urbanism circulating in Europe at the time, such as those proposed by Alison and Peter Smithson in the UK, Aldo Van Eyck in the Netherlands and Yona Friedman in France. Nevertheless in April 1959 Klein obtained sole patents for the early designs, which included the air roof as well as fire and water fountains. He also began working separately with the French architect Claude Parent, who made sketches of the wall of fire, fire and water fountains, and 'immaterial' housing. On 3 June 1959 Klein presented a lecture at the Sorbonne under the auspices of the German ambassador to France and the German cultural attaché to Paris. In this public presentation, entitled 'The Evolution of Art Towards the Immaterial', Klein traced the *Air Architecture* project back to 1951 when he visited La Granja de San Ildefonso, the summer palace of the Spanish monarchy. Though Klein paid Ruhnau homage by reciting a poem he had written in Ruhnau's honour and referred to '*our* Air Architecture manifesto', he was also sure to emphasize '*my* walls of fire and *my* walls of water'.[21] Parent, who attended the lecture, remembers the incredible energy of Klein's discourse and the magnetism of his personality. 'If he was sometimes considered barmy, it's because he was ready to do anything to be spoken about.'[22] In a text titled 'Air Architecture and Air Conditioning of Space', Klein predated '*his*' inspiration even earlier, to 1950, and tells of managing '*to persuade* Werner Ruhnau to materialize this idea of Air Architecture'.[23] Possessive when presenting his work in France, Klein was careful to be more generous when addressing a German public. In a speech delivered in Düsseldorf in January 1959 Klein stressed that he worked 'together' with Runhau.[24] This litany of conflicting assertions has to all intents and purposes demoted Ruhnau to Klein's facilitator rather than an equal partner.

During this period the pair also envisioned an updated version of the Bauhaus. The famous school, founded by Walter Gropius in 1919 to synthesize art, craft and technology, would find new life in a 'Centre of Sensibility'. Though it never materialized, Klein and Ruhnau's proposal called for a programme of artistic training that would 'reawaken the potential of creative imagination as forces of personal responsibility'.[25] The centre would have twenty 'masters' and 300 students and would cover a broad spectrum of disciplines, including sculpture, painting, architecture, theatre, television, economy, religion, politics, philosophy, criticism, film, martial arts and photography. Teachers would be experts in their field – a partial list of possible candidates included: Jean Tinguely in sculpture; Lucio Fontana, Otto Piene and Yves Klein in painting; Frei Otto and Werner Ruhnau in architecture; Claude Pascal, Pierre Henry, Sylvano Bussotti, Jacques Polieri and Mauricio Kagel in theatre; General Moshe Dayan, who had recently retired as Chief of Staff of the Israeli Defence Forces, was listed as a contender to manage the military school. Contrary to the capitalist emphasis on quantifiable material production, the centre was meant to stir the students' 'unrestrained imagination'.[26] To this qualitative end there would be neither basic requirements nor examinations, only a 'collaborative play' between teachers and students.

Apart from his close association with Werner Ruhnau, Klein also developed strong ties with Jean Tinguely. In 1952 the Swiss artist had moved from Basel to Paris and in 1955 had set up studio at the Impasse Ronsin, the small cul-de-sac in Montparnasse where Max Ernst and Constantin Brancusi also worked. In 1955 Tinguely pre-sented Kinetic sculpture in the landmark exhibition *Le Mouvement* (6–30 April) at the Galerie Denise René and met Klein when the latter's painting was rejected from the Salon. They became fast friends and in 1958 decided to collaborate on an artwork that they would both sign. *Méta-morphe sur une exaspération monochrome* (Meta-morph on a Monochrome Exasperation) would consist of a large blue monochrome painting by Klein overlaid with similarly coloured kinetic elements by Tinguely. The two artists wanted to display this work at the Salon des Réalités Nouvelles, but the jury once more refused to consider Klein's monochrome an acceptable submission. To protest this rejection, Klein and Tinguely planned to exhibit their work at a different venue with a 'delirious' and 'aggressive' introduction by Pierre Restany. They also intended to disrupt the opening of the official Salon and 'possess' the other artists' works by using flashlights to project beams of blue light on them as they strolled among the crowd. The action, *Colonization by Blue*, never went into effect as Klein had conflicting commitments at Gelsenkirchen and could not attend. 'The *Salon of False New Realities*', he wrote, 'narrowly escaped our protest'.[27] This failed tentative did not prevent them from forging on. In subsequent months, they refined their idea of collaboration to move from two superimposed elements to a cohesive whole. The result was a series of rotating blue discs affixed to electric motors that either sat on the floor, attached to shoddy wooden or metal legs made from scrap, or mounted on the wall. The discs came in a variety of sizes between 9 and 50 cm in diameter and rotated at variable rates, between 450 to 10,000 turns per minute. In November 1958 Klein and Tinguely exhibited a selection of these works in a show titled *Pure Speed and Monochrome Stability* (opened 17 November 1959) at Iris Clert's. The gallery was filled with a cacophony of noises as the motors whizzed, rumbled and clamoured and the discs hummed in turn. Following the success of their first undertaking, the two artists decided to continue working together. At this point, at least in Klein's version of events, the gap between the ideal and reality of collaboration became an insurmountable chasm.

A disagreement over a plastic tube drove them to the brink. Apparently, Tinguely did not express enough enthusiasm about

Klein's idea to circulate air of different temperatures through a tube, which led Klein to refer to this contraption as 'my machine'. This expression of ownership enraged Tinguely, who suddenly became 'quite possessive' of the concept and provoked Klein to pen a long pontification about jealousy and collaboration. Klein recalls his own brush with envy while living with Claude Pascal in Ireland in 1950. At that time, he was 'a physical man' who was mired in negative, egotistical thoughts and Pascal was 'the spirit' who reciprocated with great generosity. Drawing on this formative experience, Klein paints himself as a benevolent tutor to his headstrong friend. Referring to Tinguely as the materially motivated Hiram and himself as the spiritually inspired Solomon, his advice is to 'conquer [one's] psychological personality and become an individual and creator who says "me," "I," "my," for all belongs to him, even that which is another man's, for nothing belongs to him, not even his own life.'[28] Klein's counsel, though directed at Tinguely, could have easily applied to his own unsettled emotions and comportment when it came to the same topic. He, too, could not easily reconcile between receiving acclaim for absolute originality, sharing credit when working collaboratively with others, or acknowledging that other artists may be working with similar ideas and techniques.

Klein could easily oscillate between munificence and resentment. For example, in the very same period as he rallied to have Tinguely join the artistic team at Gelsenkirchen, he sent a panicked letter to Arman concerning a potential 'copycat'. Having learned that an unknown artist in the Midi region of France was using nude models to make artworks and exhibiting them in Cagnes, Klein sounded the alarm. 'It's serious. It must be a guy to whom I must have spoken during my holidays, after the demonstrations at Godet's in June 1958!'[29] He instructed Arman to publish an article in the local newspaper, *Nice Matin*, and assert his artistic precedence for the series of female imprints known as the *Anthropometries*.

In another case of possessive indignation, Klein sent a letter of complaint to Udo Kultermann, who had become the Director of the Schloss Morsbroich at Leverkusen, near Düsseldorf, in September 1959. In this letter Klein claimed that the term 'monochrome painting' belonged to him and demanded that Kultermann avoid using it.[30] His obsession with owning the monochrome as his cultural property is visible in two cartoons from this period, *Malevich or Space from a Distance* (1958) and *Position of Malevich in Relation to Me* (1959). In both renditions, the Russian artist is standing in front of an easel that supports a blank canvas. He holds a palette and paintbrush and gazes intently at a monochrome – presumably Klein's – which serves as his 'still-life'. Of course Klein knew that Malevich was a historical precedent that could not be willed away. However, a witty handwritten inscription on the cartoon from 1959 reveals a creative attempt to assert his originality even if was only through sheer insistence ('The real position of Malevich in Relation to Myself! Outside the phenomenology of time').

In a similar vein, Klein's relation to the Greek artist Takis, who also exhibited with Clert, was complicated by their mutual interest in levitation. Takis, who was more advanced than Klein in these investigations, exhibited three magnetic sculptures with Clert in July 1959, thus claiming absolute 'originality'. Klein learned of this 'coup' while visiting the shrine of Saint Rita in Cascia, Italy. Unable to contain himself, he wrote a letter to Clert in which he discussed an 'astonishing invention' that would free his sponges from their base and allow them to float in space. Without hidden threads or visible magnets, like Takis, he would attain 'pure levitation' by employing bursts of helium air within the hollow sponge reliefs. Klein swore Clert to secrecy, asking her to 'hide the letter' and 'not say a word to Takis . . . who would become crazy [if he found out].' Klein also notified Clert that he was sending a copy to himself to mark the date of the invention. It is here that things got tricky:

Klein predated the letter to 21 May, before the opening of Takis's exhibition, in order to prove the anteriority of his ideas. In his haste, however, he forgot that he was not at Cascia in mid-May and, more egregiously, mentioned events that occurred after this date (specifically, comments that Jean Cocteau made about his sponge reliefs, which he only exhibited in June). With this dubious document, Klein instigated a war of words that nearly cost him his friendship with Clert and left a profound frostiness between them. The final act in this drama occurred in the spring of 1960, when Clert returned from the United States. Believing that she was producing 'false Kleins', he removed all his consigned works from her gallery in her absence and threatened her with legal proceedings. One of Klein's most important partnerships came to an end in bitterness and anger.[31]

We know, too, that Klein was incensed when he learned that his proposals for *Fountains of Fire and Water* for the International Fair in New York City in 1964 were not accepted but that similar designs by a certain 'Cariuth' had been chosen instead. In anger, he wrote a letter to Mademoiselle Georges Marci, manager of Jean Larcade's Rive Droite Gallery, which began representing him after he fell out with Iris Clert in October 1960. 'The fountains of water and fire belong to me, they belong to my mythology. The battle has just begun, [I] cannot let [my] guard down and I'm already having my ideas stolen from me. I would like to be copied, but I don't want to be robbed. I want to realize things that I was the first to imagine.'[32] Unable to contain his fury, he also wrote to the renowned architect Philip Johnson in hopes that this influential figure could intercede on his behalf. Klein asked to be officially designated as 'collaborator' and 'artistic advisor' and demanded that his name be included in all publicity materials. Though he had not met Johnson when the elder statesman came through Paris and was one of the first to purchase a sponge relief from Iris Clert, he was not shy to appeal to his honour. 'I am persuaded', he wrote, 'that you would want to intervene so that I do not feel morally robbed.'[33] Johnson politely responded to Klein's letter and observed that fountains of fire and water had already been exhibited at the International Fair of 1939 and that there was nothing revolutionary about them.

Arguably the most arrant of Klein's exploits in the eyes of his detractors was his attempt to 'patent' the color International Klein Blue. Can one really claim to be the original creator of a mass-produced hue? The brouhaha has not subsided since Klein deposed a 'soleau envelope' at the National Institute of Industrial Property on 19 May 1961. As French scholar Didier Semin has shown, Klein did not patent the color blue or the binding medium, as many have claimed, but gained 'temporary protection' over his particular chemical concoction. This lesser form of assurance is only valid for five years and does not offer the same rights as a patent.[34] In the spring of 1960, while taking steps to safeguard 'his' colour, Klein was also thinking of how to ensure the continuation of his legacy by outsourcing his work to others. With Restany, Claude Pascal, Arman and film-maker Jean-Pierre Mirouze, he founded the 'International Klein Bureau'. Accorded exclusive membership, each of the core affiliates was henceforth permitted to make IKB monochromes and sign them with their own name.

Paradoxically Klein's persona of 'collaborator' dissolved at the very moment of the constitution of the movement known as Nouveau Réalisme (New Realism). This group was the brainchild of Pierre Restany, who had recently included Arman, Tinguely, Hains, Dufrêne and Klein in an exhibition titled *Les Nouveaux Réalistes* (The New Realists) at Guido Le Noci's gallery in Milan (May 1960). In the preface to the catalogue, which became the movement's first manifesto, Restany came out swinging against 'the scelorosis of established vocabularies, of all languages and of all styles'. Calling easel painting outmoded, Restany hailed 'the passionate adventure of the real perceived for itself and not

through the prism of an imaginative or conceptual transcription.'
Replacing the contemplative distance imposed by older forms of
art, the common thread that united the Nouveaux Réalistes was
their 'direct expressivity' of a 'complete sociological reality'.[35]
The exhibition in Milan was an important first step but Restany
wanted to officially launch a movement in Paris and was waiting
for a propitious moment to convene the inaugural meeting. The
Second Festival of the Avant-Garde, scheduled for 18 November
1960 at the Exhibition Palace in Versailles, was the perfect pretext.
On Thursday, 27 October 1960 at 11am, three weeks before Polieri
and Ragon's festival opened, Restany convened nine artists to
Yves Klein's apartment at 14 rue Campagne-Première. Along with
Klein, the invitees were Raymond Hains, Jacques Villeglé, François
Dufrêne, Arman, César, Jean Tinguely, Martial Raysse, Daniel
Spoerri and Mimo Rotella. César and Rotella did not turn up,
leaving a total of eight artists in attendance. A snapshot of the
meeting shows them sitting on the carpeted floor of Klein's sunlit
apartment. Raymond Hains recalls that a heated discussion ensued.
Restany was convinced that establishing a movement would bring
these young artists into the spotlight. Despite Klein's frequent lip
service to collaboration, he was wary of putting all his eggs in one
basket. Specifically he was worried that such a close association
with the rather territorial Restany would dissuade other critics
from engaging with his work. Attaching himself to this 'collective
singularity' could either strengthen him by association or subsume
his individuality. The dynamics of the discussion were highly motivated by personal affiliation and two distinct cliques formed in the
room. On the one hand were the artists from Nice: Klein, Arman
and Raysse, who banded with the Swiss: Tinguely and Spoerri. On
the other were the three 'affichistes', or poster lacerators: Hains,
Villeglé and Dufrêne. Apparently there was much back and forth
about allowing either César (in absentia) or Raysse into the group.
Another conflict emerged around the choice of name. Restany was

set on Nouveaux Réalistes while Klein preferred either Réalisme or Réalistes d'aujourd'hui (Realism or Realists of Today). Eventually, after an agreement had been reached about the movement's name, Klein passed out seven pieces of high-quality blue paper stock, one gold and one pink. Each page contained the same statement: 'Thursday, 27th of October, 1960. The New Realists realized their collective singularity. New Realism = new perceptual approaches to the real.' Though all copies were signed by each of the artists, this endorsement did not eliminate the unresolved dispute over Raysse's inclusion. Nevertheless, the very next day, Arman, Hains, Raysse, Restany and Tinguely reunited at Klein's apartment to make a collaborative work. César, Mimmo Rotella, Niki de Saint-Phalle, Christo and Gérard Deschamps joined this core group in 1961.

From the very moment of the movement's inception, the significance of incorporating such disparate artists under a common umbrella was a point of contention. Klein may have signed the declaration with his appellation 'Yves le Monochrome', but friends' testimony suggests he that was increasingly unhappy by Restany's dominant role in defining his public identity. Before joining the Nouveaux Réalistes he had sought out the critics Michel Ragon and Alain Jouffroy in hopes of a possible intellectual collaboration. Both men refused to take the artist under their wing because of their cordial relationship with Restany. Klein's departure from the group, barely a year after the declaration's signing, was precipitated by Restany's exhibition *À 40° au-dessus de Dada les Nouveaux Réalistes* (Forty Degrees above Dada, the New Realists) at the Galerie J: managed by Restany's second wife, Jeannine de Goldschmidt-Rothschild (17 May–10 June 1961). Klein was beside himself when he read the accompanying state-ment, in which the critic insisted that the Nouveaux Réalistes were the descendants of Dada. Since he was in the United States and unable to take immediate action, he wrote his old friend an uneasy letter in which his brewing disagreements were finally articulated. With extreme politeness and even a hint of humility, he insisted that he was 'not totally in agreement with forty degrees above Dada' before staunchly expressing his reservations. 'I have fought too long for my spiritual, affective, and Realist position to accept to be affiliated, in whatever manner, with Dada, whether closely or from a distance, at forty degrees above or below!!'[36] With these words, as well as a reminder that he was a co-originator of the idea, Klein tendered his resignation from the movement and asked that his work be removed from the exhibition.

The letter arrived too late and Klein's work remained on the walls. He was also included in an expanded version of the exhibition at the Rive Droite gallery, which integrated artists from the United States. Under the banner *Le Nouveau Réalisme à Paris et à New York* (New Realism in Paris and New York) Klein's work was hung in the company of Arman, César, Tinguely, Hains and Niki de Saint-Phalle as well as Jasper Johns, Lee Bontecou, Robert Rauschenberg, Varda Chryssa, Richard Stankiewicz and John Chamberlain. Still in the United States, Klein could only seethe from afar and plot his next move. On 8 October 1961, which he christened 'the day of neutral observers', he gathered Arman, Raysse, Villeglé, Hains, Dufrêne and the critics Pierre Descargues, John Ashbery, Gérald Gassiot-Talabot and Alain Jouffroy in his apartment for a ceremonial rupture from both Restany and Nouveau Réalisme.[37] The reasons for the schism were articulated in a text handed to each of the guests titled 'La Réalite depasse la fiction, le réalisme dépasse l'objet' (Reality surpasses fiction, Realism surpasses the object). Klein reiterated his disagreement with Restany's privileging of the object and his emphasis on Dada – which he termed 'abusive filiation' – in the constitution of Nouveau Réalisme.[38] The over-whelming subtext, once again, was that Klein felt he was co-initiator and co-owner of the movement and that, in fact, it was *his* art that defined the group's identity. 'It's a serious case because this movement was originally founded on Yves Klein's theories: The monochrome, blue, immaterial, void, the elements of human extra-dimensionality [sic].'[39] Arman recalls opposing Klein's stratagem with these words, which caused a rift between them for a full year: 'You are not a writer, intellectual or art critic. Analysis belongs to other people . . . It's ridiculous to be the sucessor of Breton and Surrealism, to assume the role of an art tribunal, with this attitude of policeman and priest.'[40]

Klein and Restany's creative partnership turned temporarily sour and Klein's persona as collaborator was symbolically dissolved.

8

Middle-class Mystic, 1958–62

In regard to my attempt at the immaterial, which is to say
the void . . . impossible to give you a photograph. Please publish
the photocopy, this page written by my own hand, to clearly show
that I am of good faith.[1]

Klein's spiritual affiliations are well known. As a practising
Catholic, adherent to the Cult of St Rita and adept of Rosacrucian-
ism, he stood apart from both an older generation of artists and his
own peers. In the mid-1950s, following the trauma of the Second
World War and the weakening of the bourgeois humanist tradition
and Christianity, most artists and intellectuals had embraced a
radical secularism. The dominant post-war models – Marxism,
Existentialism and Phenomenology – emphasized a wholly
materialist ethos. Klein, the 'mystic', endowed his practice with
metaphysical signification and called upon his various guardians
and ideologies to inspire, bless and protect his artwork. Though
he never renounced the material world or his taste for bourgeois
comforts he paradoxically intertwined a discourse of mysticism
with the values, symbols and desires of France's burgeoning post-
war middle class. The identity of the 'middle-class mystic' is visible
in works such as the *Anthropometries* (1958–60), *Leap into the Void*
(1960), *Fire Paintings* (1961), *Ritual Transfer of Zones of Immaterial
Sensibility* (1962) and the *Ex-voto dedicated to St Rita of Cascia* (1961).
Unpalatable to many of Klein's contemporaries, these were an

aesthetic attempt to redeem both spirituality and advanced capitalism under different terms.

Klein first performed the *Anthropometries* at a private soirée on 5 June 1958 at the house of Robert Godet on the Île St-Louis. Surrounded by approximately 40 guests, including journalists and collectors in formal evening wear, the model Marlène smeared herself in blue paint and undulated her naked body, according to the artist's precise instructions, on a piece of white paper placed on the floor. The result was a blue painting formally similar to Klein's monochromes but technically different in execution. There was nothing spontaneous about this demonstration – Klein had been working with Marlène and Claudie, the wife of Rodolphe Pichon, before this public debut. Like most of Klein's work, the twenty-minute routine met with stony silence and a suspicion that such overt eroticism crossed the limits of good taste. Klein continued this line of investigation privately for the next two years with an expanding cast of models (including Rotraut), each of whom left a unique bodily silhouette at every session. To capture this more delicate corporal trace, Klein sought a different binder from the one used in his monochrome paintings, but the sequence of events was the same: the curvaceous models covered their shoulders, chests, stomachs and thighs using IKB, the artist directed them into exact position from his perch atop a small stepladder and, once satisfied, gave them the signal to transfer their bodily imprints to paper affixed to the floor or wall.

On 23 February 1960, Klein summoned Pierre Restany and museum director Udo Kultermann to witness this new form of painting. The specific work made that day was consecrated by Restany as the 'celebration of a new anthropometric era' and was signed by all in attendance.[2] A few weeks later, on 9 March 1960, a select group of invited guests were gathered at the elite Galerie Internationale d'Art Contemporain at 253 rue Saint-Honoré. On that evening Klein's three models executed a precisely choreographed performance to the accompaniment of his one-note *Monotone Symphony*, played by classically trained musicians. Similar to John Cage's contemporaneous experimentation with the formal boundaries of music, the symphony consisted of twenty minutes of sound followed by twenty minutes of absolute silence during which the musicians stayed completely immobile. The proceedings were not a complete surprise to the gallery owner, the Comte Maurice d'Arquian, or his leading artist and counsellor, Georges Mathieu, who had been invited to a personal demonstration two days earlier, on 7 March. The rest of the well-heeled patrons were perturbed by the unfolding spectacle: each of the models emerged onto the theatrically lit proscenium with a bucket of paint and a sponge and proceeded to swathe her body in blue. In the first act, one took to the floor and writhed across the paper to create a monochrome painting while the other two stepped onto pedestals and pressed themselves against paper attached vertically to the wall to produce eight silhouettes. This was followed by a collaborative piece, titled *Dynamic Traces*, in which one model positioned herself horizontally on her belly with her legs raised in the air, while another held her arms and pulled her across the floor to leave smudged blue traces of her bust on the 'canvas'. In contrast to his models Klein was dressed to the nines in a black tuxedo, with a white bow tie and an Order of St Sebastian medal around his neck. During the 40-minute performance, he never touched or had any direct contact with his living paintbrushes.

Restany offered an interpretive matrix through which to understand the *Anthropometries*. On the invitation card to the event at the Galerie Internationale d'Art Contemporain, he made an explicit connection between Klein's 'blue gesture' and the 'anonymous handprint . . . at [the caves of] Lascaux and Altamira'. The critic claimed that both actions, though separated by 40,000 years, 'signified the awakening of man to self-awareness and the world'.[3] Klein spoke about the work in a slightly different tenor. When challenged by Georges Mathieu with the question 'what is art for you?' in a discussion immediately following the performance, Klein answered with the laconic 'Art is health!'[4] He developed a more specific explanation for the *Anthropometries* in a text titled *Le vraie devient réalité* (Truth Becomes Reality). Here, the artist claimed that his use of live models offered a wholesome equilibrium to his investigations of 'the void'. The body's 'emotional atmosphere' and its 'flesh!!!' balanced his vertiginous, lonely search for absolute pictorial space.[5] This phenomenological celebration of the body, which could easily align with contemporaneous Existentialist concerns, was also related to Klein's Christian faith and judo practice.

Klein claimed that the 'discovery' of the immaterial (or the void) was proof that he was a 'true Christian who rightly believes in the "resurrection of the bodies, in the resurrection of the flesh"'.[6] He also noted that 'the time of the brush had ended and finally my knowledge of judo was going to be useful. My models were my brushes . . . [I] devised a sort of ballet of girls smeared on a large canvas which resembled the white mat of judo contests.'[7] It is striking that Klein's renunciation of the traditional painter's tool – the brush – was couched in these terms. While artists on both sides of the Atlantic such as Jackson Pollock and Robert Rauschenberg in New York and Simon Hantai and Georges Mathieu in Paris, were taking similar steps to disconnect between the painter's hand (as a source of authentic expression) and the canvas (as the space for the articulation of his or her unique self), Klein's aesthetic exploration was distinct because of its religious connotations and its reference to Eastern rites. Though he surely knew about the Gutai Group (literally 'Embodiment'), the avant-garde group formed in Osaka, Japan, who performed a radical reassessment of painting by using their bare fee, toy cars and smashed jars of pigment, Klein took this smorgasbord of citations a step further by suggesting that Christianity would have a key role in the 'anthropophagous era' that was about to commence. He predicted that the rites of communion will be practically enacted, conjecturing that 'He who eats of my flesh and drinks of my blood will live in me and I in him.' Such a spiritually infused cannibalism would precede 'the blue era of peace and glory' in which man would harmoniously connect with 'the immaterial sensibility of the universe'.[8]

Though the pragmatic aspects of putting this credo into action were untenable, this discourse illuminates a wildly imagined concoction for a new form of utopian mysticism that merges Western, Eastern and 'primitive' semiotic codes. Despite Klein's denials, the public became wholly complicit in the objectification of the female models as voyeurs of the erotic performance of the *Anthropometries*. According to his pronouncements, the convened onlookers were meant to consume this spectacle with both religious piety ('high' Christian values) and uncivilized barbarity ('low' non-Western values). One of the most insolent aspects of the *Anthropometries* was the contrast between the models' total nudity and status as voiceless instruments in contrast to Klein's regal attire and executive power. Yet the shock of mixing high and low and Western and non-Western references was not new in the annals of the avant-garde, and neither was the self-representation of the artist as a colonizing agent: Edouard Manet's *Le Déjeuner sur l'herbe* had been equally scandalous in 1863, as had Paul Gauguin's *Spirit of the Dead Watching* in 1892, Pablo Picasso's *Les Demoiselles d'Avignon* in 1907 and Marcel Duchamp's *L.H.O.O.Q.* in 1919. Even Henri Matisse's recent cutouts, the *Blue Nudes* of 1952, had been inspired by a synthesis of influences, including African sculptures and Tahitian motifs.

The persona of the mystic would not have had the same clout, however, had it not also incited his middle-class audience to consider the issues and concerns of their day. It is perhaps Klein's nod to the recent horrors of the Second World War and the dropping of the atomic bombs in Hiroshima that complicated his affront to both traditional middle-class values and conventional modes of painting. In his diary of 1957, deliberating on the barbarism committed on the Continent and elsewhere in the name of European power, he writes, 'Europe is truly made of pure "flesh", gorged with the blood of past civilizations and speechless from inner joy. We will rapidly become anthropophagites.'[9] Elsewhere, he provocatively asks, 'Would it be better to be eaten than to be bombed?'[10] In Klein's imaginings power maintains and expands itself by annihilating and 'digesting' other national bodies. For him the ghostly silhouettes were a literal depiction of 'the shadows of Hiroshima in the desert of the atomic catastrophe' and the 'evidence of hope . . . for the survival and permanence, albeit immaterial, of the flesh'.[11] Though he was inspired by living nudes, like hundreds of artists before him Klein also incorporated the trauma of the recent past into the *Anthropometries*. The artist vehemently denied the 'erotic, porno-graphic, or amoral' dimensions of these séances.[12] Yet such an outright aesthetic exposition of France's patriarchal culture *linked* to its mobilization of technological modernism during the Second World War and its recent imperial campaigns (Indochina and Algeria) would have been much to digest. The discomfort registered on the faces of the convened audience still speaks volumes. If Klein's intentions were not immediately announced at the *Anthropometries*' premiere and only a relatively small number of people actually witnessed the event, the nude female body functioned as a discursive site around which such historical subtexts emerged in visual form. Photos and film excerpts of the soirée were diffused almost immediately by European media outlets and caused ripple waves in the avant-garde scene.

'The Anthropometries of the Blue Period', as they were dubbed by Restany, opened the door for further investigation. Klein continued to use nude models, but diversified his palette by adding pink, gold and black – applied to each living brush either separately or together. He also utilized papers of different colours, alternating between yellow, blue and pale gray. Very rarely, Klein incorporated male models into the *Anthropometries*;[13] yet this was the case in an important anthropometric work that was made to celebrate the establishment of the Nouveau Réaliste group.

The day after the declaration's signing, 28 October 1960, Arman, Hains, Restany and Tinguely came to Klein's apartment to leave their corporal mark for posterity. The resulting shroud bore the print of all five participants and was exhibited at the Second Festival of the Avant-Garde in November 1960 under the title *L'Anthropométrie collective des Nouveaux réalists* (The Collective Anthropometry of the New Realists). Another outcome was the series of *Cosmogonies* made by exposing paper with fresh paint to various weather conditions. The early works were fabricated en route from Paris to Nice, with paper installed on the roof of Klein's white Citroën. Buffeted by rain, hail, sun and wind, each 'canvas' became a testament to an inimitable meteorological moment.

Klein's interests in the signifying power of the imprint and the trace went hand in hand with a new attentiveness to the body's potential as a performative instrument. Having capitalized on the bodies of others, Klein was keen to become the central protagonist. On 19 and 25 October 1960, in a feat known as the *Leap into the Void*, he catapulted off the ledge of a one-storey building located at 3 rue Gentil-Bernard, in the Parisian suburb of Fontenay-aux-Roses. We need to backtrack ten months earlier for a full account. On 12 January 1960, Klein performed the first leap from the second story of Colette Allendy's house. He had invited Pierre Restany to witness his 'practical demonstration of levitation', but the critic was delayed and arrived late, just as the artist was returning from the event. Restany recalls that when he got there, 'Yves was tremendously excited; he was in a kind of mystical ecstasy. He truly seemed to have just accomplished some prodigious physical feat. He said to me,

"You have just missed one of the most important events of your life." He was limping slightly from a twisted ankle . . .'[14]

Since Bernadette Allain's presence was insufficient proof of Klein's exploit, Klein was spurred to perform the two additional jumps that have become legendary. What is fascinating about the first ('missed') event is Klein's insistence on the attendance of a credible witness and his judgement that it was the spectator – not him – who would experience the 'most important event' of their life. To that end, the second and third actions were documented by the duo of Harry Shunk and Janos Kender in a series of photographs that serve as the only extant visual evidence of the *Leap into the Void* and are an integral part of the artwork. Indeed, Restany did not need to show up at these subsequent jumps because the photographs served as the perfect, empirical validation of Klein's physical prowess and could impress the public at every single viewing, as if for the first time. Klein authorized two images to represent the performance. In one the street is completely deserted while in the second a lone cyclist is pedalling nonchalantly away from the viewer. The scene is slightly dreary save for the intense moment of 'drama' in the foreground: the improbable vision of an impeccably outfitted man suspended in mid-flight. The photograph was included in a one-day newspaper, *Dimanche* (Sunday), which Klein produced especially for the Second Festival of the Avant-Garde. Closely resembling the mass-circulation newspaper *Journal du Dimanche*, the Sunday edition of the Paris daily *France-Soir*, Klein's version could be picked up free of charge at the Galerie Rive Droite and at select kiosks throughout Paris on 27 November 1960. The image was placed boldly on the front page, in the right-hand corner, and was part of Klein's overall scheme for a one-day 'theatre of the void', a collective inculcation into the artist's theories. The text directly beneath the image stated that 'the monochrome, who is also a judo champion, black belt, 4th *dan*, trains regularly in dynamic levitation! (with or without a net, at risk to his life).'[15]

Klein's conviction was that he needed to physically go into space through levitation in order to paint space. This obsession with levitation, which he defined as an 'operation by which some subjects, in a state of trance or ecstasy, can elevate themselves to a certain height above the ground', is well documented.[16] Grounded in his judo practice and his esoteric beliefs, it also resonated with the wider historical field, especially the competition between the Soviets and Americans to develop a space programme in the late 1950s and early '60s. Klein made explicit reference to the Soviet launch of *Sputnik* I in *Truth Becomes Reality* and took a stand against a purely technological, positivist exploration of space. 'It is not with rockets, Sputniks, or missiles that modern man will achieve the conquest of space. That's the dream of present-day scientists who live in a romantic and sentimental state of mind that belongs to the 19th century.'[17] Though he was convinced that man will only occupy space through 'human sensibility', Klein was fully aware of the astronauts' achievements. When Yuri Gagarin declared that 'the earth has a beautiful blue colour' after completing the first manned trip in space on 12 April 1961, Klein was overjoyed. So much so that he saved a clipping detailing Gagarin's space orbit from the front page of the *New York World-Telegram* (15 April 1961) in his scrapbook next to a photograph of himself holding a blue globe (a 'planetary sculpture') that had been exhibited at Krefeld, Germany, three months earlier.[18] He not only underlined the astronaut's exhilarating testimony of seeing the earth's blue colour from space, but inserted himself as the heroic protagonist in a handwritten text. 'In 1957, Yves Klein declared that the Earth was entirely blue. Based on this theory, he created a three-dimensional Terrestrial Globe in IKB blue, making it levitate in space outside of its axis and base support in order to better see it levitate . . . 4 years later . . . in April 1961, the Astronaut Gagarin declared: "The terrestrial globe is of a deep and intense color Blue!!!"'[19]

Imitating the gravity-free conditions of outer space, the *Leap into the Void* shows Klein poised in an eternal state of climax. Most would agree that the likely conclusion of such a daredevil plunge would be certified injury. Outtakes of the event (Klein made a total of five jumps) reveal that he did not in fact leap unprotected into empty space but was actually caught in a tarpaulin held by a group of judo students. For Klein the fabrication of this image through photomontage may have been a minor detail. Yet it is precisely this reliance on the publicity potential of mass-market mechanisms such as photography that ratified Klein's position as a middle-class mystic. He was interested in neither a technical explanation nor a rational interpretation of his claim to levitation, but wanted to create the *myth* of 'the painter *of* space' as 'a man *in* space!'[20] Photography was the perfect tool: its claim to empirical veracity – capturing an instant in time in total transparency – strengthened Klein's dubious assertions about his ability to levitate. The artist was utilizing the same channels and techniques deployed by the mass media to represent, distribute and affirm images of the 'real' and, in placing *Dimanche* in newspaper kiosks, did not distinguish between art and publicity. Although Klein was making visible the 'invisible' structures through which the real was fashioned, it was not a critical demystification. On the contrary, he was perpetually adding more layers to his own personal myth, the myth of his aesthetic practice and the techniques of image production as naturalized 'truths'.

The mediated image was also an integral aspect of Klein's *Fire Paintings*, a series of 150 works begun on the last day of his exhibition at the Haus Lange in Krefeld, Germany (14–26 January 1961), and substantially developed at the Centre d'Essai de Gaz de France, the development unit of the industrial conglomerate, located just outside Paris in St-Denis (18–19 July 1961). On the opening night of his exhibition *Yves Klein: Monochrome und Feuer* (Monochrome and Fire), on the grounds of the Mies van der Rohe-designed Haus Lange, the artist presented a display of fire columns and fire walls. These incorporated exposed flames within elaborately constructed vertical and horizontal structures and necessitated the technical support of engineers from the Küppersbusch factory in Gelsenkirchen (specialists in kitchen and stove appliances), representatives at the Public Works and Gas Departments of Krefeld, and museum administrators. In his first experiment Klein exposed sheets of paper and compressed boards to the brute force of the blaze for varying amounts of time, producing charred markings of diverse intensities. A few months later, film footage from the Centre d'Essai de Gaz de France shows the smartly suited Klein gripping a giant Bunsen burner and directing it at a compressed board whose surface slowly transforms into a seared silhouette. He is accompanied by a 'Fireman', a personal friend disguised in costume for the occasion, who shoots water from an impressive hose to counteract the force of the fire and create layered halos. A few days later Klein returned for another session, this time with two nude models that reproduced the *Anthropometries* using water instead of blue paint. Their bodies moistened, they pressed their bodies onto the surface of the compressed board, allowing Klein to aim an exposed flame around them so that singed imprints were left as indexes of the event.

Writing about this project in 'The Chelsea Hotel Manifesto', Klein's rhetoric was rather exalted:

My goal is . . . to register the trace of fire which has engendered this [present-day] civilization. And this because the void has always been my constant preoccupation; and I hold that in the heart of the void as well as in the heart of man, fires are burning . . . Fire is truly one of these genuine principles that are essentially self-contradictory, being at the same time mildness and torture in the heart and origin of our civilization.[21]

It is virtually impossible to reconcile these explications with the filmic and photographic documents that capture the process of the fire paintings' production. We are confronted with a paradox that is simultaneously propelled by Klein's mythical speech and by techniques that belong to the realm of science, industry and rational thinking. The impossible synchronicity of these registers cannot be separated from the context of Klein's chosen 'theatres', namely Mies van der Rohe's internationalist-style villa and the Centre d'Essai de Gaz de France. If the former served as a museum (and may have been more receptive to the graphic display of 'nudes'), the latter was an active research laboratory (in which the 'nude' had no official place). Sensitive to such alleged distinctions, Klein played with the codes of both the culture and science industries by stressing the 'scientific' elements in Krefeld and the 'sensual' aspects at the Gaz de France. Yet in both cases Klein was not functioning in a completely 'mimetic' or wholly referential way; he was not convincingly performing the 'job' of engineer or artist as would be expected within the conventions of the social contract. His 'research' somehow belonged to no system. Through the intercession of reproducible images, which exaggerated the attributes of the trade (phallic Bunsen burner as paint brush), Klein revealed the volatility of post-war middle-class identity. Though the expectation might be that a photograph could seize the uniqueness of a person's being, his compilation of gestures suggests that identity is not intrinsic but a learned idiom, gathered from a compendium of readymade images and postures that are reproduced in various settings. What is correct for the office may not be suitable for spaces of leisure and what is proper for a research unit may not be acceptable in a museum.

In 1962, in a series of performances titled *Ritual Transfer of Zones of Immaterial Sensibility*, Klein similarly questioned whether there is an 'inner law' that guarantees an art object's value or identity. If there is a work that connects the *Ritual Transfer of Zones of Immaterial Sensibility* to previous events, like the *Epoca Blu* exhibition (1957) and *Le Vide* (1958), it was Klein's issuance of 'certificates' for the official purchase of *Zones of Immaterial Pictorial Sensibility* (1959). Like Marcel Duchamp's *Tzanck Check* (1919) and *Monte Carlo Bond* (1924), Klein was testing the limits between aesthetic and exchange values by revealing the administrative conditions and transactional economies that structure both domains. The price of Klein's *Zones*, obtainable in ten different series and increasing incrementally in value from 20 to 1280 grams of gold per lot, were 'notarized' using an official gallery stamp. In the *Ritual Transfer* Klein distinguished his constitution of aesthetic value from Duchamp's pre-war paradigm through an exaggerated ceremonial dimension. Though the certificate was the first step toward the possession of an immaterial zone, Klein stipulated that in order to become full owner, the buyer would have to burn this receipt in front of the artist and three others ('an Art Museum Director, or an Art Gallery Expert, or an Art Critic plus two witnesses'),[22] and toss the gold into a nearby body of water.

Three such *Ritual Transfers* took place in 1962, each documented in photographs. According to the art historian Denys Riout, Klein presented a buyer with two options: 'Either he remained attached to the tangible traces and conserved his "receipt," but he did not really possess the "authentic immaterial value of the work." Or he wholly played the game and deprived himself of the only concrete trace of the transaction and its possession.'[23] A third element should be added to Riout's apt description – one existing between the immaterial experience and material trace as two diametrically opposed options for ownership. The buyer was also left with a *photograph* that registered the event and, though he was not its owner, the image became a public testament to the transfer. Klein's attentiveness to the documentation of the 'ritual' reveals his understanding of the mechanisms of middle-class identity.

What he grasped, better than most, is that participants in the consumption of art were not simply motivated by unmitigated possession or abnegation of an art object. Rather, the photograph asserts the 'buyer's' presence as a decisive element in the equation and becomes an authentication of their aesthetic acumen. Just as Klein built his various personas from a conglomeration of images, he realized that the public to whom he was catering was also one that came into being in front of either a real or imagined lens.

Given Klein's faith in the mechanisms of publicity, it might appear all the more surprising that he relegated one particular object to near invisibility. The *Ex-voto Dedicated to St Rita of Cascia* is a sumptuous 'reliquary' that the artist consecrated to his lifelong guardian, the patron saint of desperate causes. Klein had undertaken two previous pilgrimages to the monastery at Cascia in the Umbrian region of Italy, the first before the opening of *Le Vide* at the Galerie Iris Clert in April 1958 and the second, with Aunt Rose, to thank the saint for securing the Gelsenkirchen Musiktheater commission in 1959. Upon his third pilgrimage, just before the closing of the exhibition in Krefeld in February 1961, Klein discreetly handed over an ex-voto anonymously to a nun at the monastery gate. It was not discovered until 1979, after an earthquake damaged the building and led to a massive process of restoration. A local painter, Armando Marocco, asked the nuns for gold leaf to fabricate new stained-glass windows and they brought out Klein's coffer from the vaults. Recognizing Klein's 'work', Marocco contacted the Milanese art dealer Guido le Noci, who alerted Pierre Restany. The piece was authenticated by Restany on 18 June 1980 and was exhibited for the first time in 2006.

This small plastic box, measuring approximately 14 x 21 x 3.2 cm, is divided into three sections: an upper one with three small compartments filled with blue powder pigment (IKB), red powder pigment (Monopink), and gold leaf (Monogold) respectively, and a lower one filled with blue powder pigment supporting three gold bars of different weight from the first four sales of his *Zones of Immaterial Pictorial Sensibility*. Between these two sections, which contained a mini triptych (or, to use religious terms, a 'Trinity') of his signature colours, he inserted a folded piece of paper containing a handwritten prayer to St Rita.[24] In this invocation Klein thanks the saint for everything that she has done for him thus far and implores her to intercede on his behalf with Jesus Christ and the Virgin Mary so that they would both 'inhabit his works', that these works 'always become more beautiful' and that he would continue to 'discover new and beautiful things in art', even if he is not always 'worthy of being a tool to construct and create Noble Beauty'. Klein also petitions the saint to protect his extant works and concepts and requests that his 'enemies become his friends', or at the very least that 'he and [his] works remain invulnerable'.[25]

Though most reliquaries contain the physical remains of a holy saint (pieces of hair, body parts, fragments of clothing), Klein's ex-voto held the fundamental materials and concepts of his artistic practice. Unlike Klein's other demonstrations of spirituality, however, he did not draw upon modern techniques of documentation or publicity as proof of the ex-voto's presence. It is a remarkable deviation from his standard procedure of conceiving art objects and events whose identity tests the boundaries between reality and image. Much ink has been spilled trying to explain Klein's mystical leanings and decipher the symbolism of the ex-voto's palette (blue, pink, gold) within the strict framework of Catholicism.[26] There have also been noteworthy attempts to link his religious and artistic vocabularies, with great emphasis placed on his interest in the immaterial as a conceptual binder between these two domains.[27] Another perspective considers the process of transubstantiation, as a key element in religious faith and aesthetic experience, for its implication of both the viewer's faith and phenomenology.[28] We might add: how does this object intersect with his well-crafted persona as a middle-class mystic during the post-war French economic boom known as the Thirty Glorious Years? In Klein's choice of raw materials – mass-produced pigments and gold ingots – he captured the tension between quantitative and qualitative products. Two of the main ingredients, the IKB and Monopink, were readily available pigments that could be produced in great quantity through an industrialized process. Klein nimbly turned them into 'specialized' or 'exclusive' merchandise by adding his special binder and offering grandiloquent pronouncements about their affective powers; gold's intrinsically rarified condition, on the other hand, made it a much sought-after commodity that functioned as a visible sign of prosperity. Klein had recently affirmed this much by demanding that buyers of the *Zones* throw gold ingots into a river to become full owners of the work. But in dematerializing gold in exchange for an immaterial art experience, one might also argue that Klein spectacularly reversed the symbolic hierarchy, rendering art more desirable than hard currency.

Since the nineteenth century, gold had become a universal currency that could be used to guarantee a country's particular tender. Following the Second World War, under the terms of the Bretton Woods Agreement, many countries fixed their exchange rate in relation to the price of the U.S. dollar, which became the de facto gold standard; yet Charles de Gaulle, president of the Fifth Republic, radically reduced France's dollar reserves as a way of staving off American power.[29] Though Klein may not have been an economist or an avid follower of international news, he understood the shifting meaning of value and the difficulty in pinpointing its precise location. The discretion with which he deposited the ex-voto reveals that the confusion between aesthetic and economic systems had been completely integrated into every aspect of a practice that did not separate between life and art. In the admixture of *quantity* (readymade pigment), now turned into rarified substance, and *quality* (gold), now transformed into a universal equivalent, Klein produced a religious object that was completely of its time. Roland Barthes' words on the nature of desire serve us well: 'To expend oneself, to bestir oneself for an impenetrable object is pure religion. To make the other into an insoluble riddle on which my life depends is to consecrate the other as a god.'[30] Perhaps more than anything else, the paradoxes of Klein's ex-voto suggested that middle-class desire could project itself onto any kind of substance and system, whether real, imagined, material or immaterial, and that this desire could itself become a mystical experience.

9

The Poet-politician:
'The Blue Revolution', 1958–61

> Wisdom, philosophy, experience, science, power, etc., are all just an
> accumulation of errors, for this represents only endless strivings to
> improve, which due to false foundations, can lead us very far and
> yet nowhere at all!!! . . . Enthusiasm is the only method of real and
> direct investigation; enthusiasm always leads to the goal, which is
> of creation . . .[1]

Though he lived through the tumultuous years of the Second
World War and the throes of decolonization in Indochina and
Algeria, it is difficult to locate signs of Klein's political commitments
in his life or work. 'Commitment' – the rallying cry of Jean-Paul
Sartre and his circle – may be a fallacious term to apply to many
of Klein's generation. These were artists whose practice carried
the imprint of their time but did not represent their experiences
in the prevailing language of the Ecole de Paris or Existentialism.
In the rare case that Klein made explicit references to contemporaneous events, his scattered political reflections take the form of
impossible or outlandish propositions. Or at least, it seems as much
if considered from a pragmatic vantage point that seeks a clear
and purposeful code of conduct for a precise and implementable
political goal.

   In an eloquent analysis by the American art critic Dore Ashton,
written five years after Klein's death on the occasion of his solo
exhibition at the Jewish Museum in 1967,

He was a reactionary in the sense that many of the young intelligentsia were reactionaries in the postwar decade; theirs was a reaction against the great wartime currents of commitment, summarized by existentialism . . . When many older French intellectuals were frantic with horror, the fevered prose accompanying the 'revolution' in the visual arts was coyly transmundane, limiting itself to exalted discussions of new cosmologies, new psychism, new infinite beyond, and new brotherhoods in some distant future in the infinite beyond where 'other' art would conquer . . . Under cover of cascades of hyperbolic prose promotion, a host of younger artists stepped out into the world of show business, bringing 'reality' to their hungry bourgeois patrons.[2]

Grouped under the banner of 'The Blue Revolution', Klein developed an eccentric vocabulary to speak of this relationship between the world and the individual, with terms like 'obligation' and 'enthusiasm' evoking the diverging directions of his thought while retreating from politics as a proper name. To call Klein a 'politician' is to reframe how politics might intersect with aesthetics and how aesthetics might be political in the years of post-war French reconstruction. It is also to imagine a new ground of political and artistic possibilities, one made visible in one of Klein's lesser known personas: the poet-politician.

Klein's 'political' interest lay in the unexpected ways that dominant systems of representation became experienced as the 'personal' and the dynamic through which the 'personal' became entwined with the infrastructure of the 'real'. At the core of this paradigm shift was Klein's emphasis on the 'qualitative', which intersected with the *affective* or sensorial kernel of the individual and nurtured a collective community that surpassed national models of identification. Most of Klein's 'political' pronouncements addressed the tensions between collective and individual identity in different political regimes. Specifically, he tailored his vision of 'The Blue Revolution' to France, the United States and Cuba and, more presciently, to a post-national art public. As his friend Jean Tinguely recalled, '[Klein] did not like collectivism, he liked a strong individual and liked contradiction. He was incapable of being political because it was not poetic enough for him.'[3] Despite Tinguely's blunt assessment, Klein's espousal of aesthetic 'collaboration' suggests that his relationship to collectivism was not so cut and dried. His interest in fabricating the paradoxical persona of the poet-politician – and his dependence on language as a primary tool – meant that his assertions were in the service of power while only making sense in the moment of their utterance.

In an unpublished *Sketch for a Technical Manifesto of the Blue Revolution,* a small component of Klein's *Overcoming the Problematics of Art* (1959), the artist defines the 'Blue Revolution' as 'striving for a transformation in the people's way of thinking and acting in the sense of individual "obligation", in quality, vis-à-vis the national collectivity, also in quality, vis-à-vis the collectivity of nations'. Though this brief statement is rather opaque, Klein was trying to formulate a model of belonging ('obligation') in which 'quality' would be the motivating force at every level of a hierarchical chain, from individual to nation, leading up to an international chamber of deputies. To make sure that his particular use of words would be legible, he added a small note explaining that, 'Obligation = Imaginative action with a sense of responsibility.'[4]

For Klein, this kind of structural transformation would give

the world an example of the order and grandeur of the French Revolution of 1789, which infused the universal ideal of 'Liberty – Equality – Fraternity' necessitated in the past but still at this time as vital as ever. With these three virtues, along with the rights of man and the individual, must be added a new law – in the democratic sense – that of 'quality'.[5]

This manuscript originally had an additional paragraph, which relates the synthesis of 'quality' to a feeling of 'enthusiasm'. Though it was eventually eliminated, Klein first stated that, 'Once in power, I want to organize a sort of Stakhanovism of enthusiasm, to stimulate individuals, each one in their domain, to a production of quality.'[6]

Like most of Klein's texts, this one is rife with frustrating question marks and blind spots. On the one hand he advocates a qualitative basis for the construction of a collectivity that respects the Declaration of the Rights of Man. Here it is the individual's internal force, his or her imagination and creativity, which becomes a motor for democratic civic responsibility and action. On the other Klein's language evokes the streamlined Taylorism of Stalin's Five Year Plan in his direct allusion to the state-programmed commitment to increased production (that is, the Stakhanovite Movement, 1935–40). From this perspective it is administrative coercion that impels the individual to participate in a new collective experiment. Klein concludes this draft by stating that 'Patriotrism must, evidently, become patriotism of the world as is already the patriotism of art.'[7] In these few passages Klein conjures a discursive universe that in many ways has been realized. He tapped into the way that art practices were shifting from the contemplation of discrete art objects – paintings and sculptures – to a greater interest on the spectator's own economy of the senses. He was certainly not alone in contributing to these shifts –Allan Kaprow was concurrently defining the multidisciplinary model for 'happenings' in the United States – but the language in which Klein framed them was unique. The 'enthusiasm' of which he speaks resonates with the dematerialization of the modernist art object and the emergence of the 'participant' as the aesthetic focal point. Though Klein was not entirely ready to do away with art objects, he was moving toward a practice in which objects were used to elicit the spectator's awareness of their own phenomenological force field. He was envisioning a world in which an allegiance (or 'patriotism') to art would form a community of like-minded individuals. Klein was also aware that this ardour, which he describes as the 'qualitative' aspect of the social bond, could easily become an exploitable commodity under different ideologies. In his writing one hears the double and inter-twined discourse of the Cold War context in which both democratic and communist economies treat the construct of the individual in divergent ways, the one affirming the individual's creativity as the basic building block of social equality and the other tapping into his or her productivity for the advancement of the collective good.

Klein's statements, taken to their most speculative and exhilarating conclusions, point to a post-national horizon in which the 'patriots of art' circulate freely, unhampered by national and ideological boundaries. The letters that Klein wrote to Dwight Eisenhower and Fidel Castro are illuminating. On 19 and 20 May 1958 Klein penned two identical letters to the president of the United States, the first in French and the second in English, with the notice that it was 'strictly confidential/ultra secret'.[8] In this missive Klein presents himself as the leader of the Blue Revolution, whose head office is at the Galerie Iris Clert.

At a time when painful events are wreaking havoc in France, my party has charged me with transmitting to you the following proposition: Instituting in France a Council of Ministers (provisionally named for the duration of three years, exclusively [selected from] among the leaders of our movement).

This Chamber of thought would be an obligatory international advisory assembly, conceived on the model of the UN, and composed of a representative from each nation recognized by the organization of the United Nations.

The French National Assembly would thus be replaced by our particular United Nations. The entirety of French powers, constituted in this way, would rest entirely subjected to the authority of the United Nations that is currently in New York.

We consider this solution likely to resolve the contradictions of our domestic politics . . .[9]

Klein ends this passage with excerpts taken verbatim from his *Sketch for a Technical Manifesto of the Blue Revolution.* He calls upon the world to take note of the grandeur of the French Revolution and its maxims of Liberty, Equality and Fraternity, and insists on the importance of adding 'Duty' to the new universal ideal.[10]

The art historians Didier Semin and Marie-Anne Sichère have noted that since the mid-1950s, various artists, including Enrico Baj, the co-founder of Arte Nucleare Movement, and the International Movement for an Imaginist Bauhaus, an avant-garde group emerging out of the break-up of COBRA that was vital to the foundation of the Situationist International, had been responding to Dwight D. Eisenhower's international survey on the question of freedom of research and scientific expression.[11] Eisenhower had launched this investigation under the aegis of the Institute of War and Peace Studies, a centre established with his sponsorship at Columbia University in 1951 to promote an understanding of the 'disastrous consequences of war upon man's spiritual, intellectual, and material progress'.[12] Klein's communication, though certainly resonating with Eisenhower's pronouncements, is more accurately contextualized within the framework of recent political events in France. The collapse of the Fourth Republic in April 1958 saw – in quick succession –– the return of General Charles de Gaulle, the establishment of the Fifth Republic and a significant change in the power dynamics of French government. The euphemistically termed 'events' in Algeria, a largely unacknowledged civil war raging since 1954, had set the stage for de Gaulle's comeback. The heroic leader of the French Resistance came out of a decade-long retirement to formulate a new constitution, one that dramatically shifted the balance of power from a parliamentary system to the executive branch. Most notably, under the constitution of the Fifth

Republic, the president was elected for a term of seven years and his cabinet could be granted exceptional powers to rule by decree for up to six months. In contrast to concentrating power in the hands of the president, Klein's 'party' proposed a new governing structure based on the concept of the individual's creative 'obligation' and an international body of delegates. Of course, Klein would be the titular 'leader' of this party, but his political vision extended beyond national boundaries and located the individual citizen within a global network of civic duty and engagement. And, if Charles de Gaulle was intent on rebuilding France's grandeur by insisting on its national uniqueness, especially in relation to the United States and the Soviet Union, Klein was imagining a broader international horizon within which French politics would constitute itself.

Another leader to whom Klein wrote a letter circa 1959 was the Cuban revolutionary Fidel Castro. Though there is no evidence that this letter was either sent or received, the draft has Klein congratulating Castro and expressing great interest in envisioning a collaborative model for artistic practice within a social collectivity.

> It is with enthusiasm that we have observed, unfortunately from afar, the success of your courageous, audacious, honest revolutionary enterprise for a better collective life, one that is rid of corruption as much as possible.
>
> With all our wishes for complete and total success, we send you . . . the result of our work, which I think will interest you.
>
> It has to do with ideas emerging from our active group of artists, architects and researchers of all kinds. We are searching for solutions to the problem of collaboration within a collectivity.[13]

The persona of the 'collaborator' was fundamental to Klein's participation in the international artistic team at the Gelsenkirchen

Musiktheater and his intimate, though fractious, partnership with Jean Tinguely. But here, in the guise of the poet-politician, Klein links his artistic activity not so much to Europe's recent past – that is, the Second World War – but rather to a radical reimagining of collective life in Cuba. It is Klein's architectural contributions and involvement in the Gelsenkirchen project, premised on the synthesis of the arts, which finally pushes him toward political reflections, however minor they may be.

Around the same time, he outlined his 'System of Evolution', an annotated schema that details his progression towards politics, the final step in his varied artistic practice.[14] It looks like this:

1. – Composition
2. – Judo
3. – Music
4. – Painting
5. – Sculpture
6. – Architecture
7. – Politics

In this world-view politics is the ultimate stage of an *artistic* evolution. While 'The Centre of Sensibility' played a formative role in Klein's persona of the 'collaborator', it was also significant for his *poetico-politico* identity. He imagined the Centre as a pedagogical institute that would nurture creativity and imagination as the 'qualitative' seeds of an individual's 'personal responsibility'.[15] Rather than focusing on external factors and achievements, what Klein qualifies as the 'decrepitude of the problematic of art, religion, and science', the Centre would concentrate on the 'non-problematic existence of man in this world'.[16] This utopian project was based on Klein's belief that the individual's inimitable imagination could be the basis for a better world. 'The imagination is realizable. It is viable', he writes. 'It should be lived at the School of Sensibility.

This will be its radiating nucleus.'[17] To achieve this vision by personal example, Klein stipulated that all teachers at the School of Sensibility would have to participate in its construction by collaborating with each other and with students. Klein's proposition that an artistic education can be a means to forging a political community and that 'sensibility' is its main pedagogical currency is prescient.

As a poet-politician, Klein tried to nurture each individual's affective, creative, imaginative, collaborative facets as a way of bringing about tangible results in the socio-political arena. He believed that by tapping into an individual's 'qualitative' force, it would be possible to correct a debased collective reality that was becoming more and more based on 'quantitative' foundations. Framing this persona within Klein's artistic practice and, more specifically, as an artistic intervention, helps situate two other letters from 1958 that would otherwise sound completely ludicrous or, at the very best, ironic. One such missive was sent to the Secretary General of the International Geophysical Year (IGY) at the United Nations.[18]

> Dear Secretary General:
> Several Summits have found fault with what different bodies of salt water have been called: Red Sea, White Sea, Black Sea, or Yellow Sea. Not one has ever been named 'Blue Sea.' I propose to let you benefit from my competence in the matter of blue, perfectly monochrome. In return for a payment to be arranged (but which must certainly cover the costs of the IKB planctomic – the coloring best adapted to this task – as well as my artistic share, I remain at the complete disposition of the I.G.Y. for this act of reparation.
> Regards,
> Yves Klein
> p.s. No danger for the red fish

Copies:
Mr Kropotkine, Academy of Sciences of the USSR
National Geographic Institute
Commander Cousteau
Mr Paul E. Victor
Professor Picard
Mr Alain Bombard
Mr Robert J. Godet
Admiral Norry (?), Chief of Staff of the Navy
Admiral Furstord of the Sea
Admiral Commander of the 6th U.S. Fleet (off Beirut)
Geographical Magazine [19]

In a second letter, addressed to the president of the
International Conference on the Detection of Atomic Explosions,
Klein asserts that the 'conscience of an artist' obligates him to
weigh in on the topic of 'atomic and thermonuclear explosions'.[20]
He writes,

> This proposition is simple: to paint in blue the A and H bombs,
> in a way and so that their eventual explosions are known not
> only by those who have complete interest in dissimulating
> the existence of the explosion or . . . in revealing it for purely
> political ends, but by all those who have the highest interest to
> be kept informed of the initiatives of this kind of perturbation
> – I mean the entire group of my contemporaries. It will suffice
> to tell me the location and number of A and H Bombs so that
> a payment can be arranged, but it must cover, whatever the
> circumstances:
>
> A) The price of colorants
> B) My proper artistic share (I will bear the burden for the
>   coloration – in blue – of all future nuclear explosions).

It is evident that we will exclude cobalt blue as ignominiously radioactive and that we will only use Klein blue, which has brought me celebrity status as you know. Although very busy with my current work and notably with the specialization of the ambience of the great opera at Gelsenkirchen, the humanitarian side of my proposition seems to deserve precedence over all other considerations. Do not think, however, that I am one of those who makes art follow matter. Quite the contrary, the disintegration of matter will give us the most extraordinary monochrome realizations that humanity – and I dare say the cosmos – will have ever known . . .

Copies:
His Holiness the Dalai Lama
His Holiness Pope Pius XII
President of the League of Human Rights
Director of the International Peace Committee
Secretary General of the United Nations
Secretary General of UNESCO
President of the International Federation of Judo
Editor-in-Chief of the *Christian Science Monitor*
Mr Bertrand Russell
Dr Albert Schweitzer[21]

In both letters, Klein links 'his' brand of colour – International Klein Blue – to 'humanitarian' propositions in the broadest sense possible. In the first he broaches the issue of shared resources (bodies of water) and in the second he tackles the most ominous threat to humanity (extinction by nuclear explosion). The lofty, sometimes zany, tone of Klein's writing should not detract from the main point: he posits the 'sensible' realm of colour as the zone in which political issues and aesthetic practice intersect. Colour, as a shared affective realm, becomes the foundation for the 'commons', a community that overcomes national politics and encapsulates all of humanity.

Though not widely publicized during his lifetime, Klein's persona of the poet-politician crystallized most vividly in the 'Blue Revolution'. At the crux of this disjointed project was a desire to dematerialize both art and politics into a common realm of the sensible. Of course, in Klein's bourgeois universe, nothing was ever devoid of self-interest and, like any savvy businessman, he expected to be acknowledged and monetarily compensated for his humanitarian contributions.

10

'The Flying Fascist', 1961

I shout it very loudly: 'KITSCH, CORN, BAD TASTE,' this is the new notion in ART. And while we are on the subject, let's forget art altogether! Great beauty is really true only if has intelligently absorbed into itself some 'AUTHENTIC BAD TASTE,' some 'EXCACERBATING AND VERY CONSCIOUS ARTIFICIALITY' with a touch of dishonesty.[1]

In the spring of 1960 Yves Klein traded allegiances when he abandoned the Galerie Iris Clert and joined the Galerie Rive Droite. His move from the small, experimental Left Bank gallery located near the Ecole des Beaux-Arts to the esteemed Right Bank institution situated in the vicinity of the Place de la Concorde heralded an absolute 'arrival' as a superstar. Having already made a name for himself as an emerging talent in France, Germany and Italy, Klein coveted American recognition. The Galerie Rive Droite's owner, Jean Larcade, and its director, Georges Marci, had strong connections to the American art scene. Through their intercession Klein had his first U.S. solo exhibition, *Yves Klein le monochrome*, at the Leo Castelli Gallery in New York City (11–29 April 1961). Debuting in the same gallery where the artists Robert Rauschenberg, Jasper Johns and Frank Stella had recently exhibited some of the most advanced work of the time was quite a coup.

What he could not foresee when he and Rotraut set off by steamship from Le Havre on 19 March 1961, was the overwhelming animosity that would await him at the end of their seven-day

Atlantic crossing. Klein's American experience was not all negative: his exhibition at the Dwan Gallery in Los Angeles (29 May–24 June 1961) was well received and he was warmly welcomed on the West Coast by the likes of Edward Kienholz and Walter Hopps, co-founders of the Ferus Gallery, Irving Blum, prominent collector of Andy Warhol's works, and artists such Ed Moses and Billy Al Bengston. It was New York City, however, that was the ascendant capital of contemporary art and the locus of artistic debates and it was here that Klein had a brief but violent encounter with the American neo-avant-garde (April–May 1961), an experience whose resonance continued to propel him even after his return to France. At the heart of the crisis was Klein's artistic embrace of the 'corny', a perversion of the prevalent category of kitsch, as well as his self-presentation as a 'phony', a persona especially concocted for an ambiguous and contested social body caught between the 'high' and 'low' currents of an accelerating mass culture.

While Klein's exhibition at the Leo Castelli Gallery was a milestone in his career, its actual makeup is still a matter of contention. According to his staunchest defenders, Pierre Restany and Rotraut, Castelli forced the artist to exhibit six vertical blue monochromes (195 x 140 cm) and one long horizontal blue monochrome (195 x 20 cm) when he had brought other works to be shown. Restany called the exhibition 'a poisoned gift' and claimed that 'Castelli made him exhibit *only* his monochrome paintings when Klein had moved beyond that kind of work five or six years before . . . It is significant when one thinks of the damage that can be done by a powerful dealer when he imposes his views on an artist.'[2] Rotraut also recalls that the show had only Klein's monochromes, although he had brought from France the piece *Ci-Gît l'Espace (Here Lies Space)* as well as obelisks, fire paintings, monogold and monopink panels, and rain and sponge works (all works *c.* 1960–61).[3] In a fascinating detail that has largely gone unnoticed, Klein sent a letter from New York to Dr Paul Wember,

Director of the Museum Haus Lange in Krefeld, in which he mentions that he held a film screening at the Leo Castelli gallery, which included footage from his recent exhibition in Germany.[4]

There is an additional whiff of intrigue surrounding Robert Rauschenberg's alleged role in determining Klein's reception. In one scenario, he was threatened by Klein's aesthetic proximity and 'sabotaged' his debut by giving Castelli an ultimatum: if any of the French artist's works were sold, both he and Jasper Johns would leave the gallery.[5] A second plotline credits him with greeting Klein in his studio in a 'warm' and 'pleasant' manner and introducing him to Johns.[6] To the most damning of these accusations, Castelli countered that he did not participate in a plot to 'sabotage' Klein and did not impose the final exhibition selection, but worked in close collaboration with the artist. 'The blue paintings', he claimed, 'were placed in the main room, creating the effect of total simplicity . . . The other works were on display in the back room.'[7] According to Ivan Karp, assistant director of the Leo Castelli Gallery from 1959 until 1969, while the monochromes 'had a certain strength about them, those plaque-like things . . . Leo and I felt that they really were not very significant.'[8] To Castelli the monochromes seemed more potent than Klein's newer works, which the gallerist deemed 'too kitschy' and placed out of sight in the back room.[9] Reports indicate that few people attended the exhibition's opening, that no monochromes were sold, and that three Sponge Sculptures were purchased.[10]

Assuming that the blue monochromes were, indeed, the exhibition's staple (a hypothesis supported by the installation photographs in the catalogue) and that, if newer works were included, they were not viewed by most visitors, it is hard to fathom what instigated the shrill tenor of Klein's reception. Most famously, the art critic Jack Kroll remarked that Klein, the latest Sugar-Dada to jet in from the Parisian Common Market is an engaging and erudite fellow who has pursued such an intensive path of arcane education, from satori to spongology that the whole question of whether or not he produced art is really beside the point . . . [He] may be called the George M. Koan of French Neo-Dada . . . [Klein's monochromes] look like cosmic blotters, or cushions from titanic sofas, or hunks of the Arcadian sky from Loew's Paradise in the Bronx.[11]

The critic Roland F. Peese Jr noted the monochrome's 'immense, almost unbearable quiet' and remarked that 'its grandeur is one of absence.' His review ends ambivalently with the observation that the 'blue of outerspace nothingness follows you, clings to the buds of your tongue, tastelessly or tastefully depending upon your tolerance for the monomania of the controversial Klein's "spiritual fluid".'[12] In subtle and not-so-subtle ways Klein's critical reception condemned him for a lack of sincerity, skill and taste and for colluding with the lowest forms of popular culture. All this seems tempered in comparison to the vitriolic personal response elicited by his interaction with the New York art scene. For instance, Billy Klüver, electrical engineer at Bell Telephone Laboratories and co-founder of EAT (Experiments in Art and Technology), recalls that Klein angered people through his incessant philosophical pontifications and references to himself and his work.[13] We also learn that Klein got into a fistfight with John Bernard Myers, the director of the Tibor de Nagy Gallery, during a dinner party at which he was repeatedly called 'the blue boy'.[14] Most hurtful to Klein was a rumoured rebuke by Mark Rothko, who apparently turned away from him without a word.[15] The art historian and critic Barbara Rose notes that Klein's silliness repelled people and had him dismissed as 'neo-Dada' and a 'phony'. Her assessment is unequivocal: 'We all thought that [he] was a

fraud.'[16] The artist Lawrence Weiner recollects that Robert
Rauschenberg would later refer to Klein as 'the flying fascist'.[17]
Even one of Klein's closest friends in the United States, the artist
Larry Rivers, observed that 'many found Klein, his work, and the
history that preceded him "difficult", "affected" and "distasteful"'.[18]
A year after his death, the enmity towards Klein did not wane.
According to the artist Donald Judd, it was his 'copious publicity'
and 'shenanigans' – not his artwork – that had elevated him to
the rank of the newest of the younger European artists.[19] Larry
Rivers tried to explain the particular hostility toward Klein in
the context of this national rivalry. 'Out of some protectionist
policy about the American art market, or the idiotic idea that
Americans are the only interesting or meaningful artists of our
time, Yves was dismissed as a European upstart whose work
was somehow derived from American art, or even worse, was an
impossibly ambitious phony.'[20]

   These personal recollections, which may be highly questionable
and should be approached with a healthy dose of scepticism,
have generally been understood as indicative of the artistic rivalry
between New York and Paris for cultural hegemony.[21] There may
be some truth to this proposition, as Klein broached the subject
in an unfinished text upon his return to France.

> Paris-New York, what does that mean today? The Ecole de Paris
> has not existed for a long time, at least not as it was determined
> in the past. For me, the past is yesterday in the same measure as
> ten years ago, twenty years ago, fifty years ago . . . The city of
> New York is no longer a place to stay, work, or be inspired, as it
> was before the war and in its immediate wake. It's nothing but
> a space of passage, a station. In the same way that a rising artist
> has to pass through Paris, whether he's American, Dutch, French
> or Japanese, he also has to pass through New York! But that
> absolutely does not mean that Paris is finished, that nothing

happens there, and that everything occurs in New York! No, it means that today we no longer have the Ecole de Paris or the New York School – there exists only the school of the entire world![22]

Klein's musings are remarkable for his understanding that a Paris–New York axis could no longer structure a contemporary art world that was in the process of becoming ever more diffuse. His radically 'internationalist' vision of a 'new world order' most likely emerged from his discouraging New York experience, which made him perceive the city as provincial and chauvinistic. It was also a tacit message to Pierre Restany, who was vigorously contributing to the rivalry between the neo-avant-garde in Paris and New York by delineating a strict difference in their use of the readymade. During Klein's sojourn in the United States, Restany organized two exhibitions that eventually led to an insurmountable breach between artist and critic: *Á 40° au-dessus de Dada* at the Galerie J (17 May–10 June 1961) and *Le Nouveau Réalisme à Paris et à New York* (New Realism in Paris and New York) at the Galerie Rive Droite (July 1961). As mentioned earlier, in these exhibitions Restany broadened the purview of Nouveau Réalisme to incorporate additional artists in France and the United States (including Robert Rauschenberg and Jasper Johns) without conferring with Klein. Equally problematic was the fact that the critic posed an intrinsic connection between Nouveau Réalisme and the readymade, a mass-produced object he claimed was central to the reconfiguration of post-war artistic practice.

Klein's ideas were not simply reactive to his surroundings. He was proactively goading both his American and French public of critics and peers by deliberately engineering and inhabiting the persona of the 'phony' on two different registers that would speak to the particularity of the local situation. He offers a crucial entry point to his inflammatory strategies in New York in 'The Chelsea

Hotel Manifesto', written in collaboration with Neil Levine and Jean Archambault while in residence at the famous hotel and presented posthumously in 1962 in an exhibition catalogue.[23] Much of the manifesto is a recycling of earlier texts announcing his accomplishments (monochrome painting, the void, sculptures of fire and water, anthropometries, air architecture, monotone symphony) and articulating his search for immaterial states. Undoubtedly he wanted to demonstrate both the scope of his achievements and the 'philosophy' that served as his catalyst, which may have been largely unknown to his American audience. As if responding directly to his critics, however, Klein also writes, 'It disturbs me to hear that a certain number of them [the young generation of artists] think that I represent a *danger* to the future of art – that I am one of those disastrous and nefarious products of our era who must be crushed and destroyed completely before the propagation of the *progress of evil* [emphasis is mine].'[24] Discussing his recent practice, and specifically the piece *Ci-Gît l'Espace*, he asserts,

> I am enthusiastically interested in 'the corney' [*sic*]. I have the feeling that there exists in the very essence of bad taste a force capable of creating something far beyond what is traditionally termed art. I want to play with human sentimentality and 'morbidism' in a cold and ferocious manner. Only recently, I have become a sort of undertaker (oddly enough, I am using the very terms of my enemies). Some of my latest works have been tombs and coffins.[25]

The word 'corny' already existed in modern English usage to express a triteness or exaggeration of sentiment.[26] First appearing in 1932, it is defined as 'of such a type as appeals to country folk; rustic or unsophisticated; tiresomely or ridiculously old fashioned or sentimental; hackneyed, trite, inferior', as well as 'exaggerated

theatricality or grandiose but commonplace sentiments'.[27]
In Klein's narrative of self-valorization, however, it was 'given
[to him] as a gift' by Marcel Duchamp during one of their two
meetings in New York.[28] In his eccentric idiolect the 'corney'
instantiates the inventive power of bad taste, a creative force
that might overcome the modernist categories of art. Its particular
significations can be teased out from *Ci-Gît l'Espace*, which he
may have exhibited at Castelli along with the blue monochromes
and which was certainly on his mind when he composed 'The
Chelsea Hotel Manifesto'. Resembling a tomb and eliciting both
attraction and repulsion, *Ci-Gît l'Espace* is made of a sunken wood
gold panel covered with mobile and fixed gold leaves, a hollow IKB
sponge-wreath and fake silk roses. Its irreproachable bad taste –
or corniness – emerges from its inappropriate combination of
romantic 'sentimentality' and pathological 'morbidism'. And
while it exists as a stand-alone art object, its thoroughly 'bad taste'
also implicates every fibre of the viewer's somatic and scopic
armature in ways that complicate the modernist claim for an
autonomous art object.

Klein's claims worked directly against Clement Greenberg's
Modernist Painting, a manifesto for a model of modernism based
on medium specificity. In the American critic's famous dictum,
'The essence of Modernism lies . . . in the use of characteristic
methods of a discipline to criticize the discipline itself, not in
order to subvert it but in order to entrench it more firmly in its
area of competence.'[29] Modernism, for Greenberg, was based
on a medium-specific practice – painting confronting its two-
dimensional condition and sculpture its three-dimensional
condition – that was equated with aesthetic autonomy and
deemed a last bastion against the incursion of mass culture.
As if to didactically demonstrate the obsolescence of this notion,
Klein documented himself activating his work, jumping over
Ci-Gît l'Espace in an acrobatic judo manoeuvre and submissively

lying underneath the piece in a staged 'death-pose'. By theatrically revealing the importance of the space below, above and around the work through such supplements (or in Donald Judd's terms 'shenanigans'), Klein made it abundantly clear that his conception of the corny implicates the 'death' of (modernist) art and the haemorrhaging of signification beyond the art object and into the receptive tastebuds of the public. Through his exaggerated showmanship, the kind that had him branded a 'phony', Klein created an unsettling disjunction between the object and its contingent conditions and effects. This disruption questioned whether a work of art could still be subversive through its autonomous internal force or whether mediating elements now played an all-powerful role in constructing signification and subjectivity.

But how does the story of kitsch fit into this? At first merely anecdotal, Klein and Rauschenberg allegedly had a heated exchange at a party organized by collector Robert Scull. To Rauschenberg's condemnation that his work was 'corny', Klein purportedly responded: 'Yes, my work is voluntarily corny, but your work is KITSCH and you don't even know it!'[30] Entertained as a serious contestation of the aesthetic field, this exchange reveals Klein's brilliant one-upmanship of his New York peers. In the essay *Avant-garde and Kitsch* (1939), Clement Greenberg famously critiqued kitsch as a 'simulacra of genuine culture', 'vicarious experience and faked sensations' and 'the epitome of all that is spurious in the life of our times'. If the avant-garde and its public represent the cultural elite who possess the critical acumen to reflect on the aesthetic production of their times, kitsch is 'the rear guard' that 'pretends to ask nothing of its customers except their money – not even their time'.[31] Kitsch is the perfect vehicle for totalitarian governments because it is 'the culture of the masses' that are hungry for easily digestible diversion. Significantly Greenberg noted that it is kitsch's inherent condition as an *object* of popular culture that makes it possible for the avant-garde to thwart its exploitation by fascist powers by counter-producing modernist objects.

Klein was called a 'phony' and worse – a 'flying fascist' – by the New York neo-avant-garde because he was regarded as distinctly right-wing in his personal life and 'belated' or 'rear guard' in his artistic one. One can imagine that in a post-war New York scene framed by Clement Greenberg's championing of a very particular strand of modernism, Klein's affinity for the regalia of the Order of St Sebastian (he provocatively wore his ornate cape and hat to the opening of his exhibition), an organization that Americans associated with royalist pretensions, and his inclusion of Republican Guards to control the crowd in attendance at the opening of *Le Vide*, a sign of the oppressive potentiality of the Republic, were considered highly suspect. Klein's penchant for judo was also viewed negatively in New York because of its associations with a militarist mentality and some lingering rumours that Klein had trained General Franco's bodyguards while teaching in Spain.[32] All this was compounded by Klein's flagrant 'showmanship', his adoration of uniforms, rituals, medals and other arcane flourishes, which did not align with the seriousness of Abstract Expressionism and its sanctification of the painterly gesture as a sincere articulation of the artist's authentic self. Though Klein's monochromes may have fit the paradigm of 'serious' neo-avant-garde art objects, he could not assert precedence in the American context since Robert Rauschenberg had created the *White Paintings* a full decade earlier in 1951 and had occupied the position of the local *enfant terrible* as early as 1955.[33] The striking visual incommensurability between the IKB monochromes and *Ci-Gît l'Espace* might have baffled the local art scene. These works seemed to belong to two different genealogies (avant-garde and kitsch), yet Klein complicated this ideological binary by framing them in discursive terms that aligned both strands with 'sensibility'.

In 1961 Klein understood better than anyone else that the Abstract Expressionists, the local vanguard that emerged in the 1940s, and Robert Rauschenberg, the very epitome of the New York neo-avant-garde of the 1950s and '60s, were still navigating the aesthetic field within a matrix of object production while a new post-object modality needed to be articulated. Though Allan Kaprow had situated the artistic event within the environment of the spectator as early as 1958, Klein's position was more complex because it also inserted the issue of 'bad taste' into the equation through his embrace of the corny.[34] He was not only contesting the paradigm of 'objecthood', which would be a key point for artists and critics alike in the coming decade, but suggesting that sensory experience was an emerging and elusive aesthetic component that could not be policed to meet the prevailing ideological criteria of taste. To make this point, he added another proverbial nail to Rauschenberg's coffin in a French-language interview. Asked whether the definition of bad taste couldn't be attributed to the American artist's works, Klein shot back: 'No, I disagree because Rauschenberg always insisted, and he even told me so during our long discussions in New York . . . that he painted and repainted the objects that he used for his works.' When the interviewer rephrases the question to detect whether a modicum of bad taste might nonetheless be detected in Rauschenberg's work, Klein replies: 'No, I think that the old academicism of paintbrush and color is present . . .'.[35] In this exchange Klein insists on Rauschenberg's fidelity to technologies of traditional art making, most notably the use of the paintbrush and, by extension, the format of easel painting. In Klein's vernacular kitsch is the discursive site for outdated painterly practices while the corny creates a new perceptual sphere for art production and consumption. Klein embraced the persona of the 'phony' in order to elicit the paroxysms of the local avant-garde and their institutional mechanisms of legitimization and support and, in this way, expose their belatedness in understanding this shift. If Klein based the corny's mandate for post-object production on his dramatis personae and vociferous linguistic claims, we cannot discount the fact that most viewers would have probably considered the art works he exhibited at Castelli as traditional 'objects' and would have branded him a 'phony' for the incongruity between the material appearance of his art and his claims for dematerialization. In Klein's defence he was simultaneously manoeuvring through a normative field of signifiers that were already in circulation while producing a second that did not yet exist.

Klein may have discounted the Paris–New York alignment as obsolete but was not bereft of his own territorial designs and loyalties. After his return from New York City, he keenly advocated for the Ecole de Nice, which he claimed was at the origin of all significant art production in Europe in the 1950s and '60s.[36] Having spent much of his childhood in the Côte d'Azur, Klein knew that the region had been home to many artists throughout the early and mid-twentieth century. Yet Klein was not thinking of artists like Henri Matisse or Pierre Bonnard, whom he would have associated with the establishment of the Ecole de Paris, but of his contemporaries, such as Arman, Ben Vautier, César and Martial Raysse. With prescient conjecture, Klein announced: 'Our vision turns towards the west where we see Los Angeles rather than New York because Los Angeles is mysterious, and I understood nothing about it, while I've surpassed New York and then there's Tokyo. I see a new art axis: Nice-Los Angeles-Tokyo; we will be joined by China.' In Klein's iteration, the Ecole de Nice was not just meant to decentralize the conventional art axis; it was also going to overturn the predominant artistic mindset. Going along with Martial Raysse's claim that the school's members were not 'prisoners to the notion of the artist', Klein stated that they were existing in a state of 'health' and 'holiday'.[37] At the crux of this designation was the issue of artistic labour, which in the early

1960s was becoming aligned with the market and elision of exchange value with aesthetic value. Klein conflated artistic work with absolute leisure – free from the structures and techniques of capitalist labour – by distinguishing between tourists and the Ecole de Nice. If tourists could only visit Nice during a leave of absence from work, the Niçois artists asserted their permanent state of leisure while making art. To further differentiate between the Niçois and everyone else (that is, the Ecole de Paris, Dada and American neo-Dada), Klein characterized his closest peers as 'vampires of the sensibility of today's world'.[38]

Klein's discourse on the Ecole de Nice developed from two distinct yet mutually constitutive threads. The first, rooted in his personal aspirations to expand beyond the autonomous parameters of Art into the realm of Life, inflected his statements on the collective goals of the Ecole de Nice:

> I want to 'be', plain and simple. I will be a 'painter.' People
> will say of me: that's the 'painter.' And I will feel myself to be
> a 'painter,' a true one precisely because I won't paint, or at least
> not in appearance. The fact that I 'exist' as a painter will be the
> most 'formidable' pictorial work of this age . . . The role of the
> painter in the society of the future will be to live 'externally,'
> to live in a collectivity in which he will refine, through his
> presence, the best, the purest, the most delicate states of
> sensibility . . .[39]

Klein uses the denominations available to him – 'painting' and 'painter' – but instils them with meanings that belong to a new order of aesthetic and social experience that does not yet have an identity but that clearly renounces the conventions surrounding traditional object production. This position was a key element in his rift with Restany, which occurred shortly after his return from New York City. In no uncertain terms he laid out the essential differences between himself and Restany in a text titled *La réalité dépasse la fiction, le réalisme dépasse l'objet* (Reality exceeds fiction, realism exceeds the object).

> As long as I was the promoter and founder [of New Realism], it wasn't the adventure of the object . . . what is the object doing in the adventure of New Realism . . . The New Realists want to create an experience of . . . impregnation in sensibility . . . In no way are they searching to provoke or shock the bourgeoisie. They share a mind-set with the Ecole de Nice: Being on vacation but not being tourists; . . . making money but not by selling their artworks . . .[40]

Klein's goal was to wrench the art object from Restany's retrospectively aimed discourse, which affiliated it with the historical avant-garde, and establish a more contemporary hermeneutic field.

Though it may not be immediately apparent, the second trigger for Klein's elaboration of the Ecole de Nice was his understanding of the value system of the New York art scene, as it appeared to him circa 1961. What he identified as his compatriot's lusty embrace of life, leisure and the realm of the sensible evolved directly from his personal distinction between the nuances circulating around the terms 'kitsch' and 'corny'. If kitsch related to object-based production, then corny would be the utter negation of such alienated labour in favour of 'sensibility' or life's open-ended vagaries. Having witnessed New York's more advanced art market, Klein realized that his idyll of 'just being' could not possibly exist outside a market system. 'Leisure' could only be transformed into 'art' if the goal of artistic production would radically shift its focus from object production to an economy of experience. In this vein, Klein described the Ecole de Nice in a witty way that was not any less serious for it: 'We like commerce, we really like money: we're not looking to sell our works to "make" money, we "make" good times.

In other words, we are a group of gangsters, the gangsters of sensibility in the world! Incidentally, in slang the "niçois" is a trickster, who makes money in strange ways.'[41]

Like a Janus-figure, Klein's persona had two dimensions: the 'Niçois' confronted the local context and distinguished between the 'traditional' object-based practice of the Ecole de Paris and that of an emerging generation of artists who were approaching art objects as potential forms of participatory experience. The 'phony' engaged with the American arena and differentiated between the competing neo-avant-gardes, a loosely affiliated group of young guns on either side of the Atlantic who were contesting the art language that preceded them and an economic market being forged around them. For both aspects of this persona, Klein relied on a strategy of trickery, which only seemed as such if one were holding onto outdated concepts and beliefs about what art should be in an a historical moment when the artistic sphere was being radically reconstituted.

11

Showman, 1961–2

To live a perpetual manifestation, to experience the permanence
of being: to be present everywhere, elsewhere, inside like outside,
a kind of sublimation of desire, a matter imbibed, impregnated
"throughout" . . . and everything continues, monotheater, beyond
  the psychological domain at last . . .[1]

In the final year of Klein's life, between the summers of 1961 and
1962, he enacted the persona of the 'showman' in two seminal
events. At his wedding to Rotraut Uecker on 21 January 1962 and
participation in *Mondo Cane (A Dog's Life)*, which had its preview
at the Cannes Film Festival on 10 May 1962, Klein's longstanding
relationship to the mediated image reached a new level of spectacularization. These two episodes, vastly different in their outcome,
stemmed from a similar impulse: a desire to construct and control
an image world that would broadcast his artistic 'presence' and
affect public opinion. From the very start of his career, Klein was
a discerning handler of the mechanisms and channels of publicity
as means of self-promotion and legitimation: he did not just practise judo in Japan in the privacy of the Kodokan Institute in 1952,
but consciously filmed himself doing it to authenticate his *judoka*
persona. Similarly the catalogue format and colour-samples-cum-
monochromes within *Yves Peintures* and *Hagenault Peintures* of
1954 were linked to both the art world's procedures of aesthetic
validation and techniques of commercial advertising. Most of his

major exhibitions and performances were extensively documented, including the double billing at the Galerie Colette Allendy and Galerie Iris Clert in 1957, the *Anthropometries* at the Galerie Internationale d'Art Contemporain in 1960 and *Fire Works* at the Gaz de France in 1961. Significantly *The Leap into the Void* of 1960, was only available as a mass-produced photographic image in the self-published newspaper *Dimanche*.[2] Klein's constant courtship of publicity in his art and life certainly did not gain him any friends among the militant left-wing avant-garde, who critiqued the insidious effects of 'spectacle culture' on contemporary French society. Yet his embrace of the visual sphere as a site for the construction of his various personas revealed that spectacle culture had already insinuated itself into all registers of subjectivity. In the case of his wedding, Klein internalized the experience of life-as-an-image in ways that permitted him to perform the most intimate aspects of his biography as a media event. With *Mondo Cane*, on the other hand, he was not be able to support this suture, which transformed this persona itself (and not his life as he knew it) into a perversity of his intentions and, some say, led to his untimely death.

Though Klein's trip to the United States was less triumphant than he had anticipated, two significant events awaited him when he returned. Following a major exhibition at the Galleria Apollinaire in Milan in November 1961, his fourth solo show that year, he learned that Rotraut was pregnant and immediately began organizing their wedding. Initially he wanted the nuptials to take place on Saturday, 20 January 1962, the feast day of St Sebastian. Since Klein had been designated a Knight of the Order of the Archers in 1956, this was a symbolically charged day and a means to ensure that most of the members of the Order, habitually scattered throughout France, would be in Paris and could attend wearing their full regalia. When the Order's strict rules made it impossible to hold a wedding on the saint's day, Klein chose to have it on Sunday, 21 January, a day on which the Catholic Church does not traditionally perform marriages. Klein choreographed every last detail of the sumptuous event, which took place at the church of St-Nicolas-des-Champs in Paris's third arrondissement. The invitation's gold, blue and pink colour palette, an allusion to Klein's most recent monochromatic production, not only cited the families of the bride and groom but also announced the attendance of the Chevaliers of the Order of St Sebastian. The film, shot by a cameraman named Albert Weill who worked for the Gaumont Film Company, captured the extravagance and pomp of the wedding ceremony, which began with a newly scored version of the *Monotone Symphony* (a wedding gift from the composer Pierre Henry) played as the couple proceeded to the altar. Rotraut's whimsical ensemble, designed by Klein, consisted of a gothic-styled white gown with matching veil, gloves and flowers and a 'medieval' International Klein Blue crown perched on her head. Her regalia was coordinated with his ceremonial dress, which included a Chevalier's cape, a sword, a plumed bicorn hat and a Maltese cross medallion. The finely arrayed processional of altar boys and Chevaliers, making their way among the hundreds of invitees, carried the insignia of the Catholic church and the Order of St Sebastian. The members of the Order surrounded the couple as they recited their vows in the candle-filled church – a long camera shot lingers on their entwined hands, followed by a quick cut to an statue of Jesus and then to a nearby Chevalier – and formed a long vaulting of crossed swords to greet them as they exited through its Romanesque portal. Interspersed shots capture Marie Raymond wearing an IKB dress and a page boy with an IKB bow tie; guests and curious strangers milled around the church before the couple was whisked by a white Jaguar, filled with white and blue flowers, to a cocktail reception at La Coupole. A late-night party followed at the studio of Larry Rivers, Klein's closest acquaintance in New York, who was temporarily residing in Paris. The next day, Klein allegedly searched the newspapers to see if his wedding had received press coverage and was disappointed to discover it had not.[3]

If most weddings are composed of ceremonial elements that 'stage' the holy union of bride and groom, Klein's showmanship took ritual to a hyperbolic dimension. By 1962 the distinction between Klein's 'personal' and 'artistic' spheres became more and more ambiguous as he embraced a universe of representation in which appearance became reality. What Klein did not realize, during the thrall of his wedding ceremony, were the consequences of this nexus. He had the illusion of being able to direct and control his own spectacularization and could not comprehend the effects it would have on his own perception of himself when he encountered his mediated persona in image form. What would happen, in other words, when Klein's image would become a free-floating signifier unmoored from his precise intentions?

Also upon his return from the United States, Klein was invited to appear in a feature-length documentary titled *Mondo Cane* that the Italian film director Gualtiero Jacopetti was making in collaboration with Paolo Cavara and Franco Prosperi of Cineriz Studios in Rome. The Italians had sought him out the previous year, but a firm contract for the artist's participation was only reached on 12 July 1961 and filming took place a few days later, on 17 and 18 July. Jacopetti asked Klein to perform a sequence of the *Anthropometries* in front of his cameras so that the world could learn about to the artist's radical inventions from monochrome paintings to 'living paintbrushes'.

Klein could not turn down such a scintillating commercial platform, even more so because he had recently felt slandered by Claude Chabrol's *Les Godelureaux* (*Wise Guys*, 1961). Even before the film was completed, he had heard that it was to include a particularly 'scandalous' sequence depicting a young artist making monochromes and conducting a séance with nude models that appeared strikingly similar to his *Anthropometries*. These rumours reached him through the grapevine since Chabrol was shooting this scene at the Galerie Iris Clert, from which Klein had recently departed under less than pleasant circumstances. Chabrol's anticipated portrayal of the crazy artist living a 'Parisian dolce vita' provoked Klein to begin legal proceedings against the director for defamation of character.[4] In a letter drafted by his lawyer, Klein accused Chabrol of a 'malicious reconstitution of certain pictorial experiences that [he] had recently presented to critical reception'.[5] To prove his case, Klein had to substantiate his invention of both monochromes and *Anthropometries.* Livid that in her sworn testimony, Iris Clert had taken credit for inspiring him to use nude female models in his painterly practice, Klein called upon Arman, Jean-Pierre Mirouze, Restany and Ruhnau to bear witness on his behalf. The deposition of evidence was a lengthy process that lasted until March 1962, by which time Chabrol's film had been released and the film-maker and Klein had allegedly become friends.[6] The newspaper *L'Express* would eventually characterize the scene in question, which lasts approximately twenty minutes, as 'a vast orgy' in which 'Mr Chabrol has been seized by debauchery.'[7] Interviewed for this article, Chabrol explained that 'At the heart of it, what I wanted to show was a dying society. A very futile universe in the process of putrefaction . . .'.[8] One can imagine Klein's ire at being made an example of such social decay despite the fact that the critical press barely referenced the scene in which he was parodied. In his dealings with the legal system the artist's only recourse to counter the fictional persona in Chabrol's film was to locate its inspiration in real life. He soon learned that this would be a lengthy process that would require the cooperation of associates and former friends and could not be managed in a timely or surefire way. The rhythms of commerce moved faster than the methods of jurisprudence and Klein realized that the impact of images had greater repercussions in the public sphere than any court testimony. It is indeed ironic that this contentious episode drove him to appear in *Mondo Cane.*

In Klein's logic, there was a better way to 'trump' the divide between 'life' and 'art'. Rather than allowing Jacopetti to fabricate an imagined artist – played by an actor who followed the director's instructions – he would hold sway over his filmic representation by appearing as himself and writing his own storyline. In a letter to his most intimate friends in New York, Larry and Clarisse Rivers, Klein bragged that 'as soon as [he] was back in Paris [he] had to begin to prepare [himself] for acting in a big movie, big screen, in Technicolor . . . It was about me, directing a big classic orchestra, playing my monotone symphonie [sic] and also directing at the same time seven beautiful nude girls painting with their bodies some hudges [sic] canvases, etc., etc.'[9] To maintain complete jurisdiction over his image, Klein submitted a precise 'scenario' that functioned as an agreement between the artist and Cineriz Studios. It stipulated the exact progression of scenes, which were to represent his aesthetic trajectory from monochromes to *Anthropometries*. It also mandated his right to final authorization over his depiction once the film was completed and before it premiered. The only artistic licence Klein gave to Cineriz Studios was to decide the exact length of the sequence after the two-day shoot at which he produced the anthropometry known as the *Suaire Mondo Cane* in 1961.[10]

Befitting the occasion, Klein and Georges Marci travelled by aeroplane to the film's premiere at the Festival de Cannes on 12 May 1962. The artist arrived at the cinema in a rented blue Rolls-Royce and a crisp tuxedo and, joined by Arman and his wife Eliane, awaited his moment of glory. Unfortunately it never came to pass, as Jacopetti had not respected the contract's terms and edited the film in ways that denigrated the integrity of Klein's practice. The original 25-minute performance was reduced to four: most of which fetishistically gorges on the nude models languishing in a bath of blue pigment; he was characterized as 'the late Czechoslovakian painter'; and the *Monotone Symphony* that initially accompanied the sequence was mostly over-dubbed with a woozy saccharine soundtrack. Even as it pretends to shed light on Klein's art, the haughty narration subtly mocks the artist and his penchant for using a single colour. 'As some of you may have guessed', the speaker divulges, 'Klein's favorite colour is blue. Blue is also his favourite form. As a matter of fact, blue is his only form and his only colour. Blue are his paintings, for which there is a great demand . . . The masterpiece, each phase of whose creation we've had privilege of recording on film, is on sale for only 4 million francs.'[11] Klein's brief appearance (subtitled 'Blue') was only a small part of Jacopetti's 'shockumentary', which consisted of eccentric, often disturbing vignettes of human and animal depravity collected in Western and non-Western cultures. Inserted among fast cuts of hyperreal 'first' and 'third' world customs, including 'primitive' peoples in New Caledonia suckling pigs and 'refined' ones in the United States consecrating cemeteries to dogs, Klein's art practice appeared as just another crass oddity. According to most biographical accounts, the shock of this depiction caused Klein to have a heart attack in his hotel room in Cannes. It was to be the first of three heart attacks that would eventually lead to his death less than a month later. Without contributing to Klein's mythology, which so often caters to such sentimental embellishments, it remains important to consider the possibility that an image could leave a serious impression on the artist. Indeed, here was a case in which 'Klein the showman', having learned from the unpleasant experience of *Les Godelureaux*, had taken every precaution to mould, perform and administer the persona he wished to broadcast for the camera. What could possibly disrupt a direct and absolute connection between his intention and the moment of reception? When he witnessed this same performance as an image that had been transformed by Jacopetti into a signifier of decadence and exploitation, he could not identify 'himself' in it. Throughout his life, Klein never felt a sense of deceit in eliding his art and life; yet transfigured into an image, he now appeared (and saw himself) as a master of counterfeit. Framed in Guy Debord's terms, one might say that Klein's confrontation with the spectacle's power to mediate and invert all aspects of life triggered a profound experience of alienation.

In an ironic turn of events, three days later Rotraut received a letter of condolences from Joan Miró for the death of her 'husband' Franz Kline, who had died on 13 May. That very same day, on 15 May, Klein was invited to participate, along with Pierre Restany and Jean Tinguely, in a public debate at the Musée des Arts Décoratifs on the theme of 'Art and Industry'. Provoked by an audience who balked at the collaborative potential between the two fields, Klein launched into a fervent denunciation of industry that only stopped at the insistence of the moderator, Eugène Claudius-Petit (a politician and advocate for urban renewal). That night, at an opening for the group exhibition *Donner à voir* at the Galerie Creuze, Klein's pallor was so unsettling that his friends tried to revive him with alcohol. When his disposition did not improve, they took him to the local hospital where he was diagnosed with a cardiac lesion and told to get as much rest as possible. Klein did not heed the doctor's advice and continued to work at fever pace, making a triptych of sponge reliefs in blue, pink and gold that required the frequent handling of polyester. His small studio apartment on the rue Campagne-Première did not have proper ventilation and he was inhaling large quantities of toxic fumes. The vapours from the polyester were so strong that they permeated every part of the building and incited his neighbors to lodge a complaint.

Friends remember that during those last weeks of May 1962, Klein was tired, morose, irritable and resigned to an early death. He was not galvanized by a new project, proposed by Albert Weill, to incorporate animal traces into his paintings. He had decided to name his unborn son Yves and charged Arman to be his godfather. He was also making preparations to leave the Galerie Jean Larcade in favour of the Galerie Karl Finker and had scheduled a meeting with its director for 7 June. To François Dufrêne he allegedly confided that 'death has given me a warning so that I can prepare myself.'[12] On the evening of 5 June, following his longstanding custom, Klein dined with Rotraut at La Coupole. The following day, 6 June, he received a number of visitors, including his father, Fred, the gallerist Jean Larcade, and his good friend Roger Cario. Not feeling well that afternoon, he called his doctor; by the time he arrived, it was too late. Yves Klein died of a heart attack on 6 June 1962 at the age of 34. He is buried alongside Marie and Rose Raymond in a small cemetery in La Colle-sur-Loup.

Klein's Afterlives

I'm telling myself, deep down, why compare that which has no reason to be with that which should be and that which is already? But does it have quality? Is it necessary? Is it true? Is it both beautiful and ugly? Is it both true and false? Is it both good and evil? Is it complete?[1]

Klein's posthumous critical reception has continued to contend with his paradoxical and performative personas, each cynical jab or hallowed praise revealing his persistent role as a provocative catalyst in the aesthetic sphere. Though more than 50 years have passed since his death, each one of Klein's 're-appearances' still goads or inflames the world of art while his myth continues to grow. The numerous responses to his practice make visible Klein's ongoing ability to agitate contemporary expectations of what artistic identity should be and to reveal the potency of particular aesthetic ideologies, tastes and value systems as framing devices of the artistic field.

When Klein died in 1962, the French and American press treated his passing very differently. Pierre Restany's support did not falter and he offered the most mythifying praise in the art journal *Cimaise*. Catapulting Klein to the impossible status of near-divinity, he wrote,

His career was marked by conquest stages that are practically myths incarnated in deeds . . . This exalted visionary projected into the present all the myths of the future. His thinking was cosmogonic; his thirst for the absolute was total. Ceding to the Promethean temptation, he directly annexed all the manifestations of the Elementary, the Wind, the Rain, the Lightning; he built on the air with the air; then he domesticated fire. His expressive urgency that was without frontiers knew no reserved domain. For Yves Klein there was no problem (physical or metaphysical), but responses . . . His legend will only grow and with it a new dimension of his immutable presence.[2]

The art critic Michel Ragon struck a more judicious note when assessing the artist's contributions.

[Klein's] beginnings attracted a lot of attention with his invention of monochrome painting, that is to say a uniformly blue surface. Hoax? We thought so at first. And when he invited art lovers to come meditate in an absolutely empty gallery, the scandal reached its apogee . . . But in these last years, we noticed that Yves Klein, though he had a certain talent for publicity, was more than a one trick pony . . . By the end, he had built a body of work full of inventions and infinitely more serious than one might think . . . [3]

The obituary in *Le Monde* concurred that he was 'the most turbulent, the most demonstrative of the Parisian avant-garde painters' but vacillated over whether his relevance would endure. 'It is not sure whether he will remain in the dictionaries. But his taste for risk and his paradoxical search for the absolute will live inscribed in the nest of his work.'[4] The American press, meanwhile, laconically noted that the 'French painter whose works included paintings in solid "Klein blue" and others made with paint covered nude women as "brushes" died in Paris of a heart attack.'[5] A year after his death, the American artist and critic Donald Judd offered this rather brutal and chauvinistic dismissal: 'although the biggest frog, he was the biggest in a rather stagnant pond. He was not as good as several of the best younger American artists, but he was a good second.'[6]

In 1967 the Jewish Museum in New York organized a solo exhibition for Klein, who was no longer a direct threat to the local avant-garde. The extreme polarity between hyper-reverence and outright malignance is startling. In the catalogue the curator Kynaston McShine describes Klein's life as a 'symbolic poetic act' and suggests that in an increasingly rational world, Klein was a 'romantic' and 'visionary' artist who 'reminds us that art does not necessarily have to be "rational" but that it can be hermetic or mystical'.[7] As is to be expected, Pierre Restany added to this glorifying dimension by calling Klein the 'latest prophet of Europe' and contending that his 'messianic influenced dominates the entire present course of artistic pursuit'. Klein, Restany professes, 'didn't paint to paint but to *reveal his truth*, the new language of art of which he was convinced he held the secret'.[8] The writer and journalist Pierre Descargues further inflated Klein's status as a sage by arguing that for him 'painting is the key to knowledge'.[9] In contrast the American press refused to accept this superhuman, quasi-divine incarnation of Klein, and went on the attack. While it was recognized that the exhibition at the Jewish Museum transformed Klein into 'as much a cult as an artist', it was felt that 'the terms "prophet" and "messiah" are being confused, as if Klein had come to us as the savior of art.'[10] What most troubled Klein's harshest critic, John Canaday, was 'the prodigious exaltation of nonsense'.

> Only acute myopia, deliberate self-delusion, profound cynicism or a chronic case of avant-garde conformism on somebody's part can account for the museum's presenting Klein to the public as anything more than an entertainer or idea man . . .

Klein was one of the best entertainers and one of the most fertile idea men in the business, but as anything more he is unacceptable.[11]

Canaday jabs his dagger deeper by disparaging Klein as one of 'the truly great vaudevillians' who 'presented as liberations of the spirit a series of tricks that are more accurately interpretable as symptoms of art's mortal illness'.[12] These jarring comments suggest that in 1967 Klein's paradoxical personas still evaded critical analysis. He was either monumentalized and mythologized in the art historical and museological narratives in impossibly heroic terms or relegated swiftly as an inconsequential – yet highly malevolent – form of entertainment.

Klein's next decisive moment of reception was in 1982, when an exhibition first organized with the support of the patron of the arts Dominique de Menil at the Institute for the Arts, Rice University, Houston, Texas, travelled to the Guggenheim Museum in New York and the Centre Georges Pompidou in Paris. By the early 1980s, as the *New York Times* noted, it was clear that Klein was a 'prefiguration of several manifestations of the 1960's and 70's, among them minimal, conceptual, environmental, body and perhaps even Pop art'.[13] Yet time and again, such accomplishments were sensationally diminished by a misunderstanding of Klein's performance of multiple aesthetic personas. To most critics these identities appeared irreconcilable with his art and the expectations of how an avant-garde artist should comport himself in the public arena. Such inadequate analyses, which refuse to consider Klein's personas as aesthetic inventions, were very common in the 1980s. In the words of the *New York Times*'s cultural correspondent, Klein was, 'a relentless self-mythologizer who saw himself as superman . . . a self-promoter, a megalomaniac hooked on his own mystique and a real – albeit minor – talent whose life and work have often inspired high twaddle from writers and have made him a cult figure in Europe.'[14] The *Village Voice* heralded Klein as the French equivalent to the German artist Joseph Beuys for his canniness at achieving 'controversial effects through a remarkable but highly suspect fusion of art object, biography, and carefully nurtured personal myth'.[15]

If such caginess may be part and parcel of the artist's popular reception, how can we make sense of the scholarly resistance to contending with Klein's aesthetic personas? One of his foremost critics, the art historian Benjamin H. D. Buchloh, has greatly contributed to the development of post-war European art and the critical parameters for its investigation. In his seminal essay 'Primary Colors for the Second Time: A Paradigm Repetition of the Neo-avant garde' (1986), Buchloh examines the re-appearance of the monochrome as an avant-gardist visual paradigm in the post-war context. Klein's clever exploitation of the link between 'art' and 'spectacle', he claims, is one of the decisive differences between the pre- and post-war treatments of the monochrome. If members of the Russian avant-garde, notably Kasimir Malevich and Aleksandr Rodchenko, focused on the processes of produc-tion, Klein turned his attention to the monochrome's 'process of reception – the audience's disposition and demands, the cultural legitimation the works are asked to perform, the institutional mediation between demand and legitimation'.[16] Buchloh has difficulties coming to terms with the 'almost schizophrenic split between Klein's pictorial production and the perceptual experience he wants it to generate'.[17] He argues that this 'split' has significant implications: modernism's holistic integrity is devalued through Klein's rendering of perceptual experience 'into an area of special-ization for the production of luxurious perceptual fetishes for privileged audiences'. Simply put, Klein is no longer subscribing to the avant-garde party line by striving to eliminate 'the bourgeois contemplative mode of perception',[18] but capitalizing on spectatorship as a marketable aesthetic commodity.

Buchloh's interpretation played a momentous role in laying the critical groundwork for important art exhibitions and scholarly investigations in the next two decades. Whether in agreement or counterpoint, the struggle to adequately grapple with Klein's personas in relation to his object production and performances has been evident in major retrospectives, as for example, at the Hayward Gallery in London (1994), the Schirn Kunsthalle in Frankfurt (2004), the Centre Georges Pompidou in Paris (2006) and the Hirshhorn Museum and Sculpture Garden in Washington, DC (2010). In their ambition to introduce Klein to new audiences and emphasize his relevance for postwar and contemporary art, the impact of these exhibitions has been double: they have continued to mythify the artist while also fostering original research. Roberta Smith of the *New York Times* astutely confronted the most recent case of Klein's idolization:

> By now, hero worship of the French artist Yves Klein . . . should be a thing of the past . . . Klein was a complicated creature, given to hyperbole, adept at self-mythology, guided by an overweening narcissism and full of contradictions. He also had great style, which gave everything he did a kind of show-biz glamour . . . We live in a period when artists who reject art objects are often turned into fetishes themselves. This has happened to Klein.[19]

For all their adulation, these exhibitions have been accompanied by catalogues showcasing writings by scholars who have expanded and complicated our understanding of his influence in a global context.[20]

This critical biography has added to the collective knowledge by suggesting a different way of interpreting the relationship between Klein's 'art' and 'life'. It has presented his shifting identities as paradoxical aesthetic inventions that were not simply shunning modernism's autonomy for an embrace of the conditions of spectacle culture or vice versa. Klein's practice – his 'art' and 'life' – was based on constantly trying to subvert static positions. His paintings did away with the age-old belief that they were unchanging objects to be contemplated by a universal spectator. He inserted paintings into the broader sphere of culture and interlaced them with the fragmentary, performative and contingent temporality of images, actions and words. In the same way Klein could not abide the thought that his identity would be unchanging and thrived in ambivalence. He envisioned different aesthetic personas that only 'came to life' in the precise moment when either the artist or spectator spoke about or enacted them. The mutability of speech and action, so dependent on context, meant that his personas were varying and inconclusive. This strategy challenged both the public and the pundits and anyone else seeking a single, definitive meaning to his art and life.

Klein also complicated the way we envision artistic identity in contemporary culture. He grasped, before many of his peers, that art and life are both made up of streams of signs and images. This meant that neither the (mythical) unity of life nor the (mythical) autonomy of the modernist art object could be sustained. In his kaleidoscopic personas he transformed the narratives and histories of his life into an aesthetic project. Approaching his biography as if it were a system of signs meant that each and every part of it could be arranged and rearranged to create different 'messages' depending on each iteration and moment of reception. His treatment of signs resonates with Roland Barthes' definition of the photographic message – paradoxical visual information that is at once self-enclosed ('*without* a code') and open to the world ('*with* a code').[21] Countless contemporary artists have followed in Klein's path, with practices nourished by the uncertain and disruptive relationship between biography and art – Gilbert and George, Tracy Emin, Jeff Koons and Ryan Trecartin, just to name a few. Conservative expectations that artists should be sincere, coherent and consistent are often foiled by practitioners who insist on instigating semantic shifts to purposefully court accusation of being tricksters, pranksters or charlatans.

By turning both life and art into so many images at his disposal, Klein severely compromised the authority of both 'reality' and 'representation' as discrete fields of knowledge. Though he believed he could manage the reception of his persona – as an image – his ultimate encounter with his own spectacularized representation at the Cannes Film Festival revealed the impossibility of doing so. Klein uncannily exploited life's translation into images and suffered from the unimaginable abstraction and alienation that went with it. His faith in attaining self-presence coupled with a celebration of the openness of images was symptomatic of the post-war desire for a world rendered whole and its impossibility. He was precariously hinged within two moments – modernism and postmodernism – that coexisted in the late 1950s and early '60s. With this rich repertoire of possibilities linked to a fragmentary notion of identity, Klein's personas continue to generate profound afterlives.

References

Introduction

1 Yves Klein, 'The Monochrome Adventure', in *Overcoming the Problematics of Art: The Writings of Yves Klein*, trans. Klaus Ottmann (Putnam, CT, 2007), p. 143.

2 Yves Klein, 'Some Excerpts from My Journal of 1957', in *Overcoming the Problematics of Art*, p. 14.

3 Yves Klein's response to Joan Miró is cited in Sidra Stich, *Yves Klein*, exh. cat. Museum Ludwig, Cologne, and Kunstsammlung Nordrhein-Westfalen, Düsseldorf (Stuttgart, 1990), p. 277, n. 73.

4 Yves Klein, 'Truth Becomes Reality', in *Overcoming the Problematics of Art*, p. 190.

5 Virginie de Caumont, 'Interview with Arman', conducted on 15 January 1981, Paris, Exhibition history (10.120), p. 7. The Menil Collections Archive, Houston, Texas.

6 Virginie de Caumont, 'Interview with Bernadette Allain', conducted on 22 May 1980, Milon-la-Chapelle, Exhibition history (10.120), p. 2. The Menil Collections Archive.

7 See Nicholas Charlet, *Les Écrits d'Yves Klein* (Paris, 2005), p. 77.

8 Klaus Ottmann argues that Restany and Klein did not see eye to eye on the relationship between Dada and Nouveau Réalisme: see *Yves Klein by Himself: His Life and Thought* (Paris, 2010), p. 339.

9 Yves Klein, 'Overcoming the Problematics of Art', in *Overcoming the Problematics of Art*, p. 45.

10 Pierre Restany, 'À Quarante Degrés au-dessus de Dada, mai 1961, Paris (2ième manifeste)' in *Avec le Nouveau Réalisme sur l'autre face de l'art* (Nîmes, 2000), p. 39.

11 Kynaston McShine, 'Yves Klein', in *Yves Klein*, exh. cat., The Jewish Museum, New York (1967), pp. 7–9.

12 Kaira M. Cabañas, *The Myth of Nouveau Réalisme: Art and The Performative in Post-War France* (New Haven, CT, 2013).

13 *Yves Klein*, exh. cat., Schirn Kusthalle, Frankfurt and Guggenheim Museum, Bilbao (Ostfildern-Ruit, 2004).

14 Peter Bürger, *Theory of the Avant-Garde*, trans. Michael Shaw (Minneapolis, MN, 1984).

15 Benjamin H. D. Buchloh, 'Theorizing the Avant-Garde', in *Art in America* (1984), p. 19.

16 Roland Barthes, 'The Photographic Message', in *Image, Music, Text*, trans. Stephen Heath (New York, 1977), pp. 15–31.

1 Living on the Axis

1 Yves Klein, 'L'Art', in *Le Dépassement de la problématique d'art et autres écrits*, ed. Marie-Anne Sichère and Didier Semin (Paris, 2003), p. 26.

2 Sidra Stich, *Yves Klein*, exh. cat., Museum Ludwig, Cologne, and Kunstsammlung Nordrhein-Westfalen, Düsseldorf (Stuttgart, 1990), p. 13.

3 Biographical information on Fred Klein is scarce and there are conflicting accounts of his genealogy; see Annette Kahn, *Yves Klein: le maître du bleu* (Paris, 2000), pp. 12–13.

4 Bernadette Allain quoted in Thomas McEvilley, Conquistador of the Void' in *Yves Klein, 1928–1962: A Retrospective*, exh. cat., Institute for the Arts, Rice University, Houston (New York, 1982), p. 22.

5 Kahn, *Yves Klein: le maître du bleu*, p. 16.

6 Marie Raymond quoted in *Marie Raymond: Retrospective 1937–1987*, exh. cat., Musée d'Art Moderne et d'Art Contemporain, Nice (1993), p. 16.

7 Marie Raymond quoted in André Bonet, *Yves Klein, Le peintre de l'infini* (Monaco, 2006), p. 38.

8 Marie Rayond quoted in Thomas McEvilly, 'Yves Klein', p. 23.

9 Kahn, *Yves Klein: le maître du bleu*, p. 24.

10 Roland Barthes, *Camera Lucida, Reflections on Photography*, trans. Richard Howard (New York, 1981), p. 10.

11 Ibid., p. 11.

12 Ibid., p. 13.

13 Ibid.

14 Kahn, *Yves Klein: le maître du bleu*, p. 32.

15 Ibid.

16 Ibid., p. 34.

17 Ibid., p. 33.

18 Claude Pascal is quoted in Stich, *Yves Klein*, p. 15.

19 Ibid.

20 According to Arman, Klein received the catalogue from Marie Raymond and passed it on to him as a birthday gift. See Arman and Tita Reut, *Yves Klein, Substitution* (Nice, 1998).

21 Kahn, *Yves Klein: le maître du bleu*, p. 48; Claude Pascal is quoted in McEvilley, 'Yves Klein: Conquistador of the Void', p. 26.

22 Thomas McEvilley, 'Yves Klein and Rosicrucianism', in *Yves the Provocateur* (New York, 2010).

23 Marie Raymond is quoted in McEvilley, 'Yves Klein: Conquistador of the Void', p. 26.

24 Roland Barthes, 'Introduction to the Structural Analysis of Narratives' [1966], in *A Barthes Reader*, ed. Susan Sontag (New York, 1982), p. 283.

25 Arman's recollections are published in Stich, *Yves Klein*, p. 18.

26 Yves Klein, 'The Chelsea Hotel Manifesto, New York, 1961', in *Overcoming the Problematics of Art: The Writings of Yves Klein*, trans. Klaus Ottmann (Putnam, CT, 2007), p. 199.

27 Ibid.

28 Ibid.

29 Klein, 'Overcoming the Problematics of Art', in *Overcoming the Problematics of Art*, p. 45.

30 Benjamin H. D. Buchloh, 'Klein and Poses', *Artforum International* (Summer 1995), pp. 94–7, 136.

2 In Search of 'Self'

1 Yves Klein, 'Utopie de l'enthousiasme', in Klaus Ottman, *Yves Klein by Himself, His Life and Thought* (Paris, 2010), p. 361.

2 Benjamin H. D. Buchloh, 'Klein and Poses', *Artforum International* (Summer 1995), p. 95.

3 Sidra Stich, *Yves Klein*, exh. cat. Museum Ludwig, Cologne, and Kunstsammlung Nordrhein-Westfalen, Düsseldorf (Stuttgart, 1990), p. 23.

4 Ibid.

5 Yves Klein, 'The Monochrome Adventure', in *Overcoming the Problematics of Art: The Writings of Yves Klein*, trans. Klaus Ottmann (Putnam, CT, 2007), p. 152.

6 Ibid., p. 154.

7 Claude Pascal is quoted in Sidra Stich, *Yves Klein*, p. 23.

8 James Shorrocks relates this information in an interview with Nan Rosenthal, 11 July 1974, Exhibition history (10.120), The Menil Collections Archive, Houston, Texas.

9 Ibid.

10 Klein is referring to the proverb from the Gospel of Saint Luke, 'You can see a mote in another's eye, but cannot see a beam in your own.' He is quoted in Annette Kahn, *Yves Klein: le maître du bleu* (Paris, 2000), p. 68.

11 Thomas McEvilly, 'Yves Klein: Conquistador of the Void', in *Yves Klein, 1928–1962: A Retrospective*, exh. cat., Institute for the Arts, Rice University, Houston (New York, 1982), p. 33.

12 Annette Kahn, *Yves Klein: le maître du bleu* (Paris, 2000), p. 68.

13 Stich, *Yves Klein*, p. 24.

14 Ibid., p. 25.

15 Ibid.

16 Ibid.

17 Kahn, *Yves Klein: le maître du bleu*, p. 75.

18 Stich, *Yves Klein*, p. 26.

19 Ibid.

20 Yves Klein, 'My Position in the Battle Between Line and Color', in *Overcoming the Problematics of Art*, p. 19.

21 Stich, *Yves Klein*, p. 26.

22 These are the tributes of Claude Pascal, Arman and Rotraut Klein, quoted in McEvilley, 'Yves Klein: Conquistador of the Void', p. 29; Sylvère Lotringer, 'Consuming Myths', in *Premises, Invested Spaces in Visual Arts, Architecture, & Design From France: 1958–1998*, exh. cat., Guggenheim Museum Soho, New York (1998).

23 Stich, *Yves Klein*, p. 26.

24 Ibid.

25 Stich, *Yves Klein*, p. 32.

26 Nan Rosenthal, 'Assisted Levitation: The Art of Yves Klein', in *Yves Klein, 1928–1962: A Retrospective*, p. 131, n. 39.

27 Stich, *Yves Klein*, p. 254, n. 49.

28 Guy Debord, *Considerations on the Assassination of Gérard Lebovici*, trans. Robert Greene (Los Angeles, 2001), p. 30.

29 McEvilley, 'Yves Klein: Conquistador of the Void', p. 35.

30 Yves Klein, 'Some (False) Foundations, Principles, Etc. and the Condemnation of Evolution', in *Overcoming the Problematics of Art*, p. 7.

31 Ibid., p. 6.

32 Kaira M. Cabañas, 'Yves Klein's Performative Realism', in *Grey Room*, 31 (Spring 2008).

33 Ibid.; Kaira M. Cabañas, 'Ghostly Presence', in *Yves Klein: With the Void, Full Powers*, exh. cat., Hirshhorn Museum and Sculpture Garden, Washington, DC, and Walker Art Center, Minnesota (2010), pp. 172–89.

34 Stich, *Yves Klein*, p. 28.

35 Ibid.

36 Yves Klein, 'Journal de Paris – La Marseillaise (26 January 1952)', in Klaus Ottmann, *Yves Klein by Himself: His Life and Thought* (Paris, 2010), p. 97.

3 Assuming the Pose

1 Yves Klein, 'On Judo', in *Overcoming the Problematics of Art: The Writings of Yves Klein*, trans. Klaus Ottmann (Putnam, CT, 2007), pp. 2 and 4.

2 Terhi Génévrier-Tausti, *L'Envol d'Yves Klein: L'origine d'une légende* (Paris, 2006), p. 50.

3 Ibid.

4 Ibid.

5 Ibid.

6 Jean Vareilles, 'Yves Klein Judoka', in *Les Fondements du judo* (Paris, 2006), p. xix.

7 Génévrier-Tausti, *L'Envol d'Yves Klein*, p. 65.

8 Sidra Stich, *Yves Klein*, exh. cat., Museum Ludwig, Cologne, and Kunstsammlung Nordrhein-Westfalen, Düsseldorf (Stuttgart, 1990), p. 34.

9 *Yves Klein*, exh. cat., Centre Georges Pompidou, Paris (1983), p. 301.

10 Stich, *Yves Klein*, p. 34.

11 Annette Kahn, *Yves Klein: le maître du bleu* (Paris, 2000), p. 96.

12 Stich, *Yves Klein*, p. 35.

13 Ibid., pp. 35–6.

14 Ibid.

15 Ibid., p. 37.

16 Kahn, *Yves Klein: le maître du bleu*, p. 108; Stich, *Yves Klein*, p. 39.

17 Kahn, *Yves Klein: le maître du bleu*, p. 108.

18 Stich, *Yves Klein*, p. 34.

19 Ichiro Abé, 'Preface', in *Les Fondements du judo* (Paris, 2006), p. 16.

20 Stich, *Yves Klein*, p. 34 and p. 255, n. 74.

21 Ibid., p. 255, n. 75.

22 Interview between Pierre Restany and Dominique de Menil, 6 December 1980, p. 1: Menil Collections Archive, Houston, Texas.

23 Interview between Claude Pascal and Virginie de Caumont, 4 May 1981, p. 2: Menil Collections Archive.

24 Stich, *Yves Klein*, p. 42.

25 Kahn, *Yves Klein: le maître du bleu*, p. 118.

26 Ibid., p. 119.

27 Ibid., p. 121.

28 Mark Cheetham, 'Matting the Monochrome: Malevich, Klein, and Now', *Art Journal*, LXIV/4 (Winter 2005), p. 7.

29 Ibid., p. 102.

30 Stich, *Yves Klein*, p. 17.

31 Cheetham, 'Matting the Monochrome', p. 10.

4 'Painter'

1 Yves Klein, 'The Monochrome Adventure', in *Overcoming the Problematics of Art: The Writings of Yves Klein*, trans. Klaus Ottmann (Putnam, CT, 2007), p. 147.

2 Denys Riout, *La Peinture monochrome: histoire et archéologie d'un genre* (Nîmes, 2003), p. 18.
3 Klein, 'The Monochrome Adventure', p. 138.
4 Ibid., p. 139.
5 Ibid.
6 Ibid.
7 Sidra Stich, *Yves Klein*, exh. cat. Museum Ludwig, Cologne, and Kunstsammlung Nordrhein-Westfalen, Düsseldorf (Stuttgart, 1990), p. 58.
8 Ibid., p. 59.
9 Annette Kahn, *Yves Klein: le maître du bleu* (Paris, 2000), p. 130.

5 Avant-garde Artist

1 Yves Klein, 'The Monochrome Adventure', in *Overcoming the Problematics of Art: The Writings of Yves Klein*, trans. Klaus Ottmann (Putnam, CT, 2007), p. 170.
2 Yves Klein, 'Text for the Exhibition *Yves Peintures* at Lacoste Publishing House, Paris, 15 October 1955', in *Overcoming the Problematics of Art*, p. 12.
3 Ibid.
4 Sidra Stich, *Yves Klein*, exh. cat. Museum Ludwig, Cologne, and Kunstsammlung Nordrhein-Westfalen, Düsseldorf (Stuttgart, 1990), p. 258, n. 37.
5 Henry Périer, *Pierre Restany, l'alchimiste de l'art* (Paris, 1998), pp. 9–47.
6 Ibid., p. 47.
7 André Bonet, *Yves Klein: le peintre de l'infini* (Monaco, 2006), pp. 93–4.
8 Yves Klein, 'The Monochome Adventure', in Ottmann, *Overcoming the Problematics of Art*, p. 154.
9 Ibid.
10 Stich, *Yves Klein*, p. 257, n. 26.
11 Pierre Restany, 'La Minute de vérité, février, 1956, Paris', in *Avec le Nouveau Réalisme sur l'autre face de l'art* (Nîmes, 2000), pp. 54–5.
12 Ibid.
13 Ibid.
14 Ibid.

15 Bernadette Allain, 'Propositions monochromes du peintre Yves', *Couleurs*, 15 (1956), pp. 25–7.

16 Ibid.

17 Yves Klein, 'My Position in the Battle between Line and Color', in *Overcoming the Problematics of Art*, p. 20.

18 Klein, 'Text for the Exhibition *Yves Peintures* at Lacoste Publishing House, Paris, 15 October 1955', p. 12.

19 Stich, *Yves Klein*, p. 79.

20 Ibid.

21 Yves Klein, 'The Monochrome Adventure', pp. 140–41.

22 Stich, *Yves Klein*, p. 260, n. 33.

23 Ibid., p. 89.

24 Annette Kahn, *Yves Klein: le maître du bleu* (Paris, 2000), p. 178.

25 Yves Klein is quoting Gaston Bachelard in 'Discours à la commission du théâtre de Gelsenkirchen', in *Le Dépassement de la problématique d'art et autres écrits*, ed. Anne-Marie Sichère and Didier Semin (Paris, 2003), p. 74.

26 Ibid., p. 73.

27 Yves Klein, 'Lecture at the Sorbonne', in *Overcoming the Problematics of Art*, p. 73.

28 Kahn, *Yves Klein: le maître du bleu*, p. 158.

29 Stich, *Yves Klein*, p. 259, n. 7.

30 Yves Klein, 'L'Aventure Monochrome', in *Le Dépassement*, ed. Sichère and Semin, p. 233.

31 Rosalind Krauss, *A Voyage on the North Sea: Art in the Age of the Post-medium Condition* (London, 2000).

32 Pierre Restany, 'L'Epoca blu, il secondo minuto della verita', in *Avec le Nouveau Réalisme sur l'autre face de l'art*, p. 56.

33 Dino Buzzatti's newspaper article 'Blu, Blu, Blu', is published in Denys Riout, *Yves Klein: L'aventure monochrome* (Paris, 2006), p. 110.

34 Ibid., p. 111.

35 Thierry de Duve, 'Yves Klein or the Dead Art Dealer', *October 49* (Summer 1989).

36 Yves Klein, 'The Monochrome Adventure', p. 145.

37 Stich, *Yves Klein*, p. 81.

6 Charlatan

1 Yves Klein, 'Lecture at the Sorbonne', in *Overcoming the Problematics of Art: The Writings of Yves Klein*, trans. Klaus Ottmann (Putnam, CT, 2007), p. 76.

2 Pierre Restany, 'Invitation Card', in Sidra Stich, *Yves Klein*, exh. cat. Museum Ludwig, Cologne, and Kunstsammlung Nordrhein-Westfalen, Düsseldorf (Stuttgart, 1990), p. 91.

3 Nan Rosenthal, 'Assisted Levitation', in *Yves Klein, 1928–1962: A Retrospective*, exh. cat., Institute for the Arts, Rice University, Houston (New York, 1982), pp. 106–10.

4 Nan Rosenthal makes these observations in 'The Blue World of Yves Klein', PhD dissertation, Harvard University, 1976, pp. 181–2.

5 Edouard Adam relates this information in an interview with Virginie de Caumont, 24 February 1981, exh. hist. (10. 120), The Menil Collections Archive, Houston, Texas.

6 Yves Klein, 'Notes on Certain Works Exhibited at Galerie Colette Allendy', in *Overcoming the Problematics of Art*, p. 23.

7 Jean Dubuffet, 'Honneur aux valeurs sauvages' [1951], trans. Kent Minturn in *RES*, *46* (Autumn 2004), pp. 259–65; Yves Klein, 'Remarques sur quelques oeuvres exposées Chez Colette Allendy', in *Le Dépassement de la problématique de l'art et autres écrits*, ed. Marie-Anne Sichère and Didier Semin (Paris, 2003), p. 54.

8 Ibid.

9 Iris Clert is quoted in Denys Riout, *Yves Klein: L'aventure monochrome* (Paris, 2006), p. 41.

10 Ibid.

11 Kaira M. Cabañas, 'Yves Klein en France: un paradoxe spatial', in *Yves Klein: corps, couleur, immatériel*, exh. cat., Centre Georges Pompidou (Paris, 2006), p. 175.

12 Guy Debord, *The Society of the Spectacle*, trans. Donald Nicholson-Smith (New York, 1994), p. 12.

13 Sidra Stich, *Yves Klein*, exh. cat. Museum Ludwig, Cologne, and Kunstsammlung Nordrhein-Westfalen, Düsseldorf (Stuttgart, 1990), p. 261, n. 58.

14 Rodolphe Pichon conveys this information in Annette Kahn, *Yves Klein: le maître du bleu* (Paris, 2000), p. 184.

15 Personal communication with Denise René, 2002.

16 Klein, 'Notes on Certain Works Exhibited at Galerie Colette Allendy', p. 22.

17 Louis-Paul Favre, 'Périple', *Combat*, 20 May 1957, p. 7.

18 Stich, *Yves Klein*, p. 98; M. R. Schnir, *Masques et visages* (June 1957).

19 Ibid.

20 *Le Monde*, 31 May 1957, p. 8.

21 Pierre Restany, *Yves Klein le monochrome* (Paris, 1974), p. 46.

22 Kaira M. Cabañas, 'Ghostly Presence', in *Yves Klein: With the Void, Full Powers*, exh. cat., Hirshhorn Museum and Sculpture Garden, Washington, DC (2010), pp. 174–89.

23 Annette Kahn, *Yves Klein: le maître du bleu* (Paris, 2000), p. 189.

24 Rotraut Uecker, '1957', www.rotraut.com, 16 June 2013.

25 Kahn, *Yves Klein: le maître du bleu*, p. 203.

26 Yves Klein, 'Preparation and Presentation of the Exhibition on 28 April 1958 at the Galerie Iris Clert', in *Overcoming the Problematics of Art*, p. 48.

27 In an undated letter to his Aunt Rose (May 1958), Klein writes that 500 to 600 people attended the gallery each day. The letter from the Gaspérini archive is cited in Stich, *Yves Klein*, p. 267, n. 30.

28 Klein, 'Preparation and Presentation of the Exhibition on 28 April 1958 at the Galerie Iris Clert', p. 49.

29 Ibid., p. 50.

30 Ibid.

31 Ibid., p. 53.

32 Interviews by Sidra Stich with Jean-Pierre Mirouze, 1 December 1991, Paris; Bernadette Allain, 30 December 1991, Paris; and Charles Le Moing, 3 December 1991, Paris, in Stich, *Yves Klein*, p. 266, n. 13.

33 Klein, 'Preparation and Presentation of the Exhibition on 28 April 1958 at the Galerie Iris Clert', p. 52.

34 Jean Grenier, 'Arts-Spectacles', *Preuves 88* (June 1958).

35 'Manifestaton d'avant-garde à la Galerie Iris Clert', *Combat* (5 May 1958), p. 7.

36 'Vernissage d'un mur blanc', *Le Figaro*, 29 April 1958; untitled article, *Aux Écoutes*, 16 May 1958.

37 These passages are quoted in Henri Périer, *Pierre Restany: l'alchimiste de l'art* (Paris, 1998), p. 105.

38 Ibid.

39 Denys Riout, *Yves Klein: manifester l'immatériel* (Paris, 2004).

40 Benjamin H. D. Buchloh, 'Plenty or Nothing: From Yves Klein's Le Vide to Arman's Le Plein', in *Premises: Invested Places in Visual Arts, Architecture, and Design from France: 1958–1998*, exh. cat., Guggenheim Museum Soho, New York (1998), p. 92.

41 Ibid.

42 Yves Klein, *Comment et pourquoi, en 1957*, unpublished document. Yves Klein Archives.

43 Yves Klein, 'Speech Delivered after the Opening Reception for the Pneumatic Period', in *Overcoming the Problematics of Art*, p. 97.

44 Kristin Ross develops the connection between decolonization and the French obsession with cleanliness in *Fast Cars, Clean Bodies: Decolonization and the Reordering of French Culture* (Cambridge, 1995), pp. 71–122.

45 Guy Debord, 'L'Absence et ses habilleurs', *Internationale situationniste*, 2 (December 1958), p. 7.

7 Collaborator

1 Yves Klein, 'Speech Delivered on the Occasion of the Tinguely Exhibition in Düsseldorf (January 1959)', in *Overcoming the Problematics of Art: The Writings of Yves Klein*, trans. Klaus Ottmann (Putnam, CT, 2007), p. 62.

2 Sidra Stich, *Yves Klein*, exh. cat. Museum Ludwig, Cologne, and Kunstsammlung Nordrhein-Westfalen, Düsseldorf (Stuttgart, 1990), pp. 107–30.

3 *Deutsche Bauzeitung: Fachzeitschrift Für Architektur und Bautechnik*, January–December 1960, p. 686.

4 'Letter from Yves Klein to Werner Ruhnau, Thursday, November 1957', in *Wie das Gelsenkirchener Blau auf Yves Klein Kam: Zur Geschichte der Zusammenarbeit zwischen Yves Klein und Werner Ruhnau*, exh cat., Museum Wiesbaden, Wiesbaden (2004), p. 41.

5 Ibid., p. 42.

6 'Letter from Werner Ruhnau to Yves Klein, November 21, 1957', in *Wie das Gelsenkirchener Blau auf Yves Klein Kam*, p. 42; 'Letter from Werner

Ruhnau to Yves Klein, November 29, 1957', in *Wie das Gelsenkirchener Blau auf Yves Klein Kam*, p. 44.

7   Yves Klein, 'Speech Delivered on the Occasion of the Tinguely Exhibition in Düsseldorf (January 1959)', pp. 62–3.

8   François Masure, 'État et identité nationale. Un rapport ambigu à propos des naturalisés', in *Journal des Anthropologues* (2007), pp. 39–49.

9   Michael Robert Marrus and Robert O. Paxton, *Vichy France and the Jews* (Stanford, CA, 1995), pp. 343–4.

10 Jean-Paul Sartre, 'Qu'est-ce qu'un collaborateur?', in *La République Française*, New York, August 1945, reprinted in the collection *Situations III* (Paris, 1949), pp. 43–61.

11 See, for example, De Gaulle's Address of 3 November 1959, quoted and translated in Roy C. Macridis, ed., *De Gaulle, Implacable Ally* (New York, 1966), p. 134: 'The Great Powers need to unite on the basis of cooperation in which each carries its own load, rather than on the basis of integration in which peoples and governments find them-selves deprived of their roles and responsibilities.'

12 Nan Rosenthal, 'The Blue World of Yves Klein', PhD dissertation, Harvard University, 1976, p. 216.

13 Michael Kelly, 'The View of Collaboration during the Après-Guerre', in *Collaboration in France: Politics and Culture during the Nazi Occupation, 1940–1944*, ed. Gerhard Hirschfeld and Patrick Marsh (New York, 1989), pp. 239–52; Herbert Lottman, *L'Épuration* (Paris, 1986); Robert Aron, *Histoire de l'épuration* (Paris, 1967–75); Peter Novick, *The Resistance versus Vichy* (New York, 1968).

14 Yves Klein, 'The Evolution of Art Towards the Immaterial: Lecture at the Sorbonne, 3 June 1959', in *Overcoming the Problematics of Art*, pp. 71–98.

15 Yves Klein, *Le Dépassement de la problématique de l'art*, ed. Marie-Anne Sichère and Didier Semin (Paris, 2003), p. 103.

16 Helmuth de Haas, 'Der Bau ist Bühne: Das Neue Theater in Gelsenkirchen', in *Die Welt*, 3 April 1959.

17 Werner Ruhnau, *Der Raum, Das Spiel, und Die Künste*, exh. cat., Musiktheater im Revier, Gelsenkirchen (2007), p. 152.

18 Yves Klein, 'Air Architecture and Air Conditioning of Space', in *Yves Klein: Air Architecture*, ed. Peter Noever and François Perrin, exh. cat., MAK Center for Art and Architecture, Los Angeles (2004), p. 97;

François Perrin, 'Air Architecture Imagination and Matter', in *Yves Klein: Air Architecture*, p. 11.

19 Yves Klein, 'It is by Staying in One's Place that One can be Everywhere', in *Yves Klein: Air Architecture*, ed. Noever and Perrin, p. 30; Yves Klein and Werner Ruhnau, 'Project for an Air Architecture', in *Overcoming the Problematics of Art*, p. 174.

20 Ibid.

21 Yves Klein, 'The Evolution of Art Towards the Immaterial: Lecture at the Sorbonne, 3 June 1959', in *Overcoming the Problematics of Art*, p. 97.

22 Annette Kahn, *Yves Klein: le maître du bleu* (Paris, 2000), p. 256.

23 Klein, 'Air Architecture and Air Conditioning of Space', p. 97 (my italics).

24 Yves Klein, 'Speech Delivered on the Occasion of the Tinguely Exhibition in Düsseldorf (January 1959)', p. 64.

25 Ibid., p. 68.

26 Ibid.

27 Yves Klein, 'Pure Velocity and Monochrome Stability, an Account of the Exhibition in collaboration with Jean Tinguely at Galerie Iris Clert', in *Overcoming the Problematics of Art*, p. 31.

28 Ibid., p. 35.

29 Kahn, *Yves Klein: le maître du bleu*, p. 241.

30 *Le Dépassement de la problématique de l'art et autres écrits*, ed. Anne-Marie Sichère and Didier Semin (Paris 2003), p. 339.

31 Kahn, *Yves Klein: le maître du bleu*, pp. 261–4.

32 Ibid., p. 349.

33 Ibid., p. 350.

34 Didier Semin, *The Painter and his Model on Deposit*, trans. Brian Holmes (Geneva, 2001).

35 Pierre Restany, 'Les Nouveaux Réalistes, April 16, 1960, Milan (first manifesto)', in *Avec le Nouveau Réalisme sur l'autre face de l'art* (Nîmes, 2000), p. 38.

36 Kahn, *Yves Klein: le maître du bleu*, p. 312.

37 Yves Klein, 'The Truth About New Realism', in *Overcoming the Problematics of Art*, p. 176.

38 Ibid.

39 Kahn, *Yves Klein: le maître du bleu*, p. 313.

40 Arman and Tita Reut, *Yves Klein, Substitution* (Nice, 1998), p. 60.

8 Middle-class Mystic

1 Yves Klein, 'With Regard to My Attempt at the Immaterial', drafted on a loose sheet of paper in the Yves Klein Archives and published in *Overcoming the Problematics of Art: The Writings of Yves Klein*, trans. Klaus Ottmann (Putnam, CT, 2007), p. 207.

2 Annette Kahn, *Yves Klein: le maître du bleu* (Paris, 2000), p. 280.

3 Henry Périer, *Pierre Restany: l'alchimiste de l'art* (Paris, 1998), p. 148.

4 Sidra Stich, *Yves Klein*, exh. cat. Museum Ludwig, Cologne, and Kunstsammlung Nordrhein-Westfalen, Düsseldorf (Stuttgart, 1990), p. 175.

5 Yves Klein, 'Truth Becomes Reality, Yves the Monochrome, 1960', in *Overcoming the Problematics of Art*, p. 185.

6 Ibid., p. 186.

7 Stich, *Yves Klein*, pp. 171–2.

8 Yves Klein, 'Truth Becomes Reality, Yves the Monochrome, 1960', p. 189.

9 Yves Klein, 'Quelques extraits de mon journal de 1957', in *Yves Klein* (Paris, 1969), p. 75.

10 Yves Klein, 'The Chelsea Hotel Manifesto', in *Overcoming the Problematics of Art*, p. 196.

11 Klein, 'Truth Becomes Reality, Yves the Monochrome, 1960', p. 187.

12 Yves Klein, '*Dimanche*', in *Overcoming the Problematics of Art*, p. 113.

13 Stich, *Yves Klein*, p. 270, n. 34.

14 Pierre Restany is quote in Thomas McEvilley, 'Conquistador of the Void', in *Yves Klein, 1928–1962: A Retrospective*, exh. cat., Institute for the Arts, Rice University, Houston (New York, 1982), p. 64.

15 Yves Klein, '*Dimanche*', p. 105.

16 Stich, *Yves Klein*, p. 217.

17 Yves Klein, 'Truth Becomes Reality, Yves the Monochrome, 1960', p. 191.

18 Stich, *Yves Klein*, p. 276, n. 51.

19 Henry Shapiro, 'Gagarin Hints He'd Like to Fly One of New Red Moonships', *New York World Telegraph*, CXXXVIII/189 (15 April 196), in *Yves Klein: USA* (Paris, 2009), pp. 118-19.

20 Klein, '*Dimanche*', p. 106.

21 Klein, 'The Chelsea Hotel Manifesto', pp. 195–6.

22 Yves Klein, 'Ritual for the Relinquishment of the Immaterial Pictorial
    Sensibility Zones', in *Overcoming the Problematics of Art*, p. 182.
23 Denys Riout, *Yves Klein: manifester l'immatériel* (Paris, 2004), p.102.
24 The entire contents of Yves Klein's letter are published in *Yves Klein*,
    exh. cat., Centre Georges Pompidou, Paris (1983), pp. 245–6.
25 Ibid.
26 Alain Buisine, 'Blue, Gold, Pink: The Colors of the Icon', in *Yves Klein:
    Long Live the Immaterial* (Nice, 2000), pp. 17–34.
27 Camille Morineau, 'le bleu, l'or et le rose: comment appropriation
    rime avec sublimation', in *Yves Klein: corps, couleur, immatériel*, exh.
    cat. Centre Georges Pompidou, Paris (2006), pp. 156–63.
28 Riout, *Yves Klein: manifester l'immatériel*.
29 Sophie Cras, 'De la valeur de l'oeuvre au prix du marché: Yves Klein à
    l'épreuve de la pensée économique', in *Marges: revue d'art contemporain*,
    11 (November 2010).
30 Roland Barthes, 'The Unknowable', in *A Lover's Discourse: Fragments*,
    trans. Richard Howard (New York, 1978), p. 135.

9 The Poet-politician

1 Yves Klein, 'Some (False) Foundations, Principles, etc., and the
   Condemnation of Evolution', in *Overcoming the Problematics of Art:
   The Writings of Yves Klein*, trans. Klaus Ottmann (Putnam, CT, 2007),
   pp. 5–8.
2 Dore Ashton, 'Art as Spectacle', *Arts Magazine* (March 1967), p. 44.
3 Jean Tinguely, 'Un Superbon camarade', in *Yves Klein*, exh. cat., Centre
   Georges Pompidou, Paris (1983), p. 254.
4 Yves Klein, 'Esquisse du manifeste technique de la révolution bleue',
   in *Le Dépassement de la problématique de l'art et autres écrits*, ed.
   Anne-Marie Sichère and Didier Semin (Paris, 2003), p. 98.
5 Ibid.
6 Ibid., p. 352, n. 16.
7 Ibid., p. 98.
8 Yves Klein, 'The Blue Revolution, Letter to Eisenhower, 20 May 1958',
   in *Overcoming the Problematics of Art*, p. 25.
9 Ibid., pp. 25–6.

10 Ibid., p. 26.

11 Sichère and Semin, ed., *Le Dépassement de la problématique de l'art et autres écrits*, p. 337, n. 1.

12 Dwight D. Eisenhower, quoted website for Arnold A. Salzman Institute for War and Peace, www.siwps.com, accessed 24 June 2013.

13 Yves Klein, 'Letter to Fidel Castro', in *Le Dépassement de la problématique de l'art et autres écrits*, ed. Sichère and Semin, p. 338.

14 Yves Klein, 'My System of Evolution', in *Overcoming the Problematics of Art*, p. 67.

15 Yves Klein, 'Creation of a Center of Sensibility', in Ottmann, *Overcoming the Problematics of Art,* p. 68.

16 Ibid.

17 Ibid.

18 Yves Klein, 'The Blue Sea, Letter to the Secretary General of the International Geophysical Year', in *Overcoming the Problematics of Art,* p.27.

19 Ibid.

20 Yves Klein, 'Blue Explosions, Letter to the International Conference for the Detection of Atomic Explosions', in *Overcoming the Problematics of Art*, p. 28.

21 Ibid.

10 'The Flying Fascist'

1 Yves Klein, 'Truth Becomes Reality', in *Overcoming the Problematics of Art: The Writings of Yves Klein*, trans. Klaus Ottmann (Putnam, CT, 2007), pp. 189–90.

2 Pierre Restany is quoted in an article entitled 'Yves Klein's Blue Carpet', by Luisa F. Flynn in *Art World*, VII/3 (December 1982).

3 Personal interview with Rotraut Klein-Moquay, New York, 25 October 2005.

4 *Yves Klein: USA* (Paris, 2009), p. 198.

5 Sidra Stich, *Yves Klein*, exh. cat., Museum Ludwig, Cologne, and Kunstsammlung Nordrhein-Westfalen, Düsseldorf (Stuttgart, 1990), p. 236 and p. 275, n. 28.

6 Interview with Rotraut Klein-Moquay, conducted by Robert Pincus-Witten and published in *Yves Klein: USA* (Paris, 2009), p. 7.

7 Castelli's recollections are published in Flynn, 'Yves Klein's Blue Carpet', p. 2, and in Stich, *Yves Klein*, p. 275, n. 20.

8 Interview with Ivan C. Karp, conducted by Paul Cummings, at the Leo Castelli Gallery, 12 March 1969. Archives of American Art. Smithsonian Institution, Washington, DC.

9 Stich, *Yves Klein,* p. 275, n. 20.

10 François Mathey, the Director of the Musée des Arts Décoratifs, recalls the lack of people at the opening and notes that instead of the customary post-opening dinner, a small group, including Klein, Rotraut, Larry Rivers and a friend, went to a Chinese restaurant. See Stich, *Yves Klein*, p. 275, n. 26. Sidra Stich notes that no works were sold in *Yves Klein*, p. 235, while, Ivan C. Karp recalls that a few monochromes were sold at a modest price. Interview with Ivan C. Karp, conducted by Paul Cummings, at the Leo Castelli Gallery, 12 March 1969. Archives of American Art. Smithsonian Institution, Washington, DC, p. 33. Robert Pincus-Witten, *Yves Klein: USA*, p. 44.

11 Jack Kroll, review of Castelli exhibition, *Art News*, LX/3 (May 1961), pp. 14–15.

12 Roland F. Peese Jr, review of Castelli exhibition, *Art International*, V/6 (June–August 1961), p. 98.

13 In a souvenir that Billy Klüver dictated to his assistant, he remembers talking to Jean Tinguely and telling him that he had stayed up till 1am because he 'got into this huge intellectual argument with Yves'. Tinguely responded, 'If you are to be with Yves you must understand how he is, and how you will always be trapped into such an argument or discussion.' Text provided by Julie Martin, New York, 27 October 2005.

14 Arman relays this information in an interview with Sidra Stich, *Yves Klein*, p. 276, n. 29.

15 Thomas McEvilley, 'Yves Klein: The Conquistador of the Void', in *Yves: The Provocateur* (New York, 2010), p. 171.

16 Personal communication with Barbara Rose, New York, 16 October 2005.

17 This anecdote about Robert Rauschenberg is related by Lawrence Weiner in a personal communication, New York, 7 December 2005.

18 The recollections of Larry Rivers can be found in 'Blues for Klein',
    ARTnews, vol. LXV (February 1967), pp. 32–3 and 75–6.

19 Donald Judd, article in 'New York Exhibitions: In the Galleries,
    Arts Magazine, XXXVII/4 (January 1963), pp. 48–9.

20 Rivers, 'Blues for Klein', p. 76.

21 Serge Guilbaut, *How New York Stole the Idea of Modern Art: Abstract
    Expressionism, Freedom and the Cold War*, trans. Arthur Goldhammer
    (Chicago, IL, 1983).

22 Yves Klein, 'Manifeste de l'Hotel Chelsea' (unpublished extract),
    in *Le Dépassement de la problématique de l'art et autres écrits*,
    ed. Anne-Marie Sichère and Didier Semin (Paris, 2003), pp. 416–17.

23 'The Chelsea Hotel Manifesto' was published in a catalogue
    accompanying the exhibition *Yves Klein* at the Gallery Alexandre
    Iolas in New York (5–24 November 1962).

24 Yves Klein, 'The Chelsea Hotel Manifesto', in *Overcoming the
    Problematics of Art*, p. 194.

25 Ibid., p. 195.

26 According to the *Oxford English Dictionary*, the first appearance of the
    word 'corny' dates to 1932 in relation to a style of musical delivery
    ('the bounce of the brass section . . . has degenerated into a definitely
    "corny" and staccato style of playing'); it reappears in 1937, also in
    relation to music ('she began to play a melody which . . . had been
    popular in the early post war days . . . "corny old stuff", said Mercer');
    it then shows up in 1944 in relation to comedy ('He wondered what
    corny gag Old Abey had thought up this time') and in 1951 in relation
    to the theatre ('Grown insolent and fat on cheesy literature and corny
    dramas'); in 1957 it speaks of art ('The Walker Art Gallery houses
    some of the corniest Victorian and Edwardian masterpieces') while
    in 1958 it refers to emotional states ('My affections are, to use a corny
    phrase, otherwise engaged'). *Oxford English Dictionary*, 2nd edn
    (Oxford, 1989), p. 949.

27 Ibid.; *Webster's 3rd International Dictionary* (Springfield, MA, 1981),
    pp. 508–09.

28 Personal communication with Rotraut Klein-Moquay, New York,
    25 October 2005. Marcel Duchamp's diary from April 1961 shows a
    notation for a meeting with Yves Klein at 9am on Thursday, 6 April,
    and the opening of Klein's exhibition at the Leo Castelli gallery on

11 April. See Rotraut Klein-Moquay and Robert Pincus-Witten, *Yves Klein USA* (Paris, 2009), pp. 116–17.

29 Clement Greenberg, 'Modernist Painting', was first broadcast on the radio as part of the *Forum Lectures* (Washington, DC: Voice of America), 1960; an unrevised version was published in *Arts Yearbook*, 4 (1961); and a slightly revised version was published in *Art and Literature* (Spring 1965).

30 Georges Marci in a letter to Sidra Stich, *Yves Klein*, p. 275.

31 Clement Greenberg, 'Avant-Garde and Kitsch', in *Clement Greenberg: The Collected Essays and Criticism*, vol. I, ed., John O'Brian (Chicago, IL, 1988), pp. 5–22.

32 Interview with Larry Rivers in Stich, *Yves Klein*, p. 275, n. 24.

33 A review of Robert Rauschenberg's exhibition at Egan notes that 'Bob Rauschenberg, *enfant terrible* of the New York School, is back again to even more brilliant effect . . .'. *ARTnews*, LIII/9 (January 1955), p. 47.

34 A review of Allan Kaprow's exhibitions at Hansa states that '[he] installed a distinct audio-visual novelty: cut out strips from about three feet to a few inches wide, suspended from almost ceiling to almost floor or less made of shower-curtain and other synthetic, as well as pure, fabrics, some transparent and splashed with paint in parody of decoration; tinfoil, crushed cellophane and Christmas tree lights added to the variety. As one wove at leisure among the even rows, one had phantasmal glimpses of other visitors doing the same – that is, absorbing courteously, with every available nerve, the sensation of being abstracted from the ordinary world to one where musique? is as concrete (?) as abstract art, and both are heroically anti-Muzak.' *ARTnews*, LVII/3 (May 1958), p. 14.

35 Klein is in conversation with Sacha Sosnowsky, reprinted in *Yves Klein*, exh. cat., Centre Georges Pompidou, Paris (1983), pp. 263–4.

36 Ibid.

37 Ibid.

38 Ibid.

39 Yves Klein, 'The Monochrome Adventure', in *Overcoming the Problematics of Art*, pp. 147–9.

40 Ibid., pp. 313–14.

41 *Yves Klein*, exh. cat., Centre Georges Pompidou, Paris (1983), p. 264.

11 Showman

1 Yves Klein, 'Dimanche,' in *Overcoming The Problematics of Art: The Writings of Yves Klein*, trans. Klaus Ottmann (Putnam, CT, 2007), p. 104.

2 François Albera, 'Yves Klein au Cinema', in *1895. Mille huit cent quatre-vingt-quinze*, no. 49 (2006).

3 Annette Kahn, *Yves Klein: le maître du bleu* (Paris, 2000), p. 378.

4 François Albera mentions a typewritten version of a no longer existing text, hand-written by Klein in October 1960, in which the artist describes his negative portrayal in Chabrol's film. Albera, 'Yves Klein au Cinema', note 21.

5 Ibid., p. 114.

6 Ibid., p. 119.

7 Ibid., p. 111.

8 Ibid., p. 112.

9 Letter from Yves Klein to Larry and Clarisse Rivers, Paris, 27 July 1961, published in *Yves Klein: USA* (Paris, 2009), p. 165.

10 Ibid., p. 106.

11 *Mondo Cane*, Gualtiero Jacopetti, Cineriz Studio, 1961, film.

12 Kahn, *Yves Klein: le maître du bleu*, p. 393.

Klein's Afterlives

1 Yves Klein, 'Dialogue with Myself', in *Overcoming the Problematics of Art: The Writings of Yves Klein*, trans. Klaus Ottmann (Putnam, CT, 2007), p. 203.

2 Pierre Restany, 'Yves Klein (1928–1962)', in *Cimaise*, IX/60 (July–August 1962), p. 84.

3 Michel Ragon, 'Yves Klein est morte', in *Arts* (Paris), 873 (13–19 June 1962), p. 11.

4 Michel Conil-Lacoste, 'Yves Klein', in *Le Monde*, 9 June 1962, p. 17.

5 *ARTnews*, LXI/4 (Summer 1962), p. 9.

6 Donald Judd, article in 'New York Exhibitions: In the Galleries', *Arts Magazine*, XXXVII/4 (January 1963), pp. 48–9.

7 Kynaston McShine, 'Yves Klein', in *Yves Klein*, exh. cat., The Jewish Museum, New York (1967), p. 7.

8 Pierre Restany, 'Yves Klein: Latest Prophet of Europe', in *Yves Klein*, exh. cat., The Jewish Museum, New York (1967), p. 11.

9 Pierre Descargues, 'Yves Klein', in *Yves Klein*, exh. cat., The Jewish Museum, New York (1967) p. 26.

10 'Klein Retrospective', *Morning Sun*, 12 February 1967; John Canaday, 'I Got the Yves Klein Blues', *New York Times*, 5 February 1967.

11 Ibid.

12 Ibid.

13 Grace Glueck, 'Art: Yves Klein Show at the Guggenheim', in *New York Times*, 19 November 1982.

14 Ibid.

15 Roberta Smith, 'Parts and Sums', *Village Voice*, 7 December 1982.

16 Benjamin H. D. Buchloh, 'The Primary Colors for the Second Time: A Paradigm Repetition of the Neo-avant-garde', in *October*, 37 (Summer 1986), p. 48.

17 Ibid., p. 49.

18 Ibid., p. 50.

19 Roberta Smith, 'Painting Thin Air, Sometimes in Bright Blue', *New York Times*, 3 June 2010, p. C24.

20 *Yves Klein*, exh. cat. Schirn Kunsthalle, Frankfurt (2005); *Yves Klein: Corps, Couleur, Immatériel*, exh. cat., Centre Georges Pompidou, Paris (2006); *Yves Klein: With the Void Full Powers*, exh. cat., Hirshhorn Museum and Sculpture Garden,Washington, DC, and Walker Art Center, Minneapolis (2010).

21 Roland Barthes, 'The Photographic Message', in *A Barthes Reader*, ed., Susan Sontag (New York, 1982), p. 198.

Select Bibliography

Klein's Writings

'Des Bases (fausses), principes et condemnation de l'évolution',
in *Soulèvement de la jeunesse*, 1 June 1952
Les Fondements du judo (Paris, 1954)
'Propositions monochroms du peintre Yves', interview by Bernadette
Allain, *Couleurs* (Paris, 1956), p. 15
'Meine Stellung im Kampf zwischen Linie und Farbe', *Zero 1* (April 1958)
'L'Évolution de l'art vers l'immatériel', paper given at a conference at the
Sorbonne, 3 June 1959, available on two 33 rpm records (Paris, n.d.)
Le Dépassement de la problématique de l'art (La Louvière, 1959)
'Mes idées sur la peinture', *Geijustu-Shincho* (Tokyo, July 1960)
'Yves Klein, l'Homme qui a vendu du vide', interview by Pierre
Descargues, *Tribune de Lausanne* (30 October 1960)
Dimanche, Le journal d'un seul jour (Paris, 27 November 1960)
'Le Vrai devient réalité', *Zero 3* (July 1961)
— and Werner Ruhnau, 'Projekt einer Luft-Architektur', *Zero 3* (July 1961)
— and Pierre Restany, 'Climatisation de l'espace', *Antagonismes II: L'Objet*,
exh. cat., Musée des Arts Décoratifs, Paris (1962)
— and Neil Levine and John Archambault, 'Due to the fact that . . .',
Yves Klein, exh. cat., Alexander Iolas Gallery, New York (1962)
Le Dépassement de la problématique de l'art et autres écrits, ed. Marie-Anne
Sichère and Didier Semin (Paris, 2003)
Overcoming the Problematics of Art: The Writings of Yves Klein, trans. and
intro. by Klaus Ottmann (Putnam, CT, 2007)
Yves Klein: Works/Writings, trans. and intro. by Klaus Ottmann
(Barcelona, 2009)

Other Relevant Works

Alison, Jane, ed., *Colour After Klein*, exh. cat., Barbican Art Gallery, London (2005)

Banai, Nuit, 'Yves Klein: The Midcult Manager of Kitsch', in *Kitsch: History, Theory, Practice*, ed. Monica Kjellman-Chapin (London, 2013)

——, 'Avant-garde or Civil Service? Yves Klein, Werner Ruhnau and The European Situation' in *Europa! Europa? European Avant-Garde and Modernism Series*, ed. Sascha Bru (Berlin, 2010)

——, 'Rayonnement and the Readymade: Yves Klein and the End of Painting', *RES: Anthropology and Aesthetics*, 51 (Spring 2007)

——, 'From the Myth of Objecthood to the Order of Space: Yves Klein's Adventures in The Void', in *Yves Klein*, exh. cat., Frankfurt Schirn Kunsthalle (2004)

——, 'Monochromatic Interventions: Yves Klein and the Utopia of Spectacular Sensibility', in *Colour After Klein: Rethinking Colour in Modern and Contemporary Art*, exh. cat., Barbican Art Gallery, London (2005)

——, 'Dangerous Abstraction: Klein in New York, 1961–1967', in *Yves Klein: Corps, couleur, immatériel*, exh. cat., Centre Georges Pompidou, Paris (2006)

Bertrand-Dorléac, Laurence, *L'Ordre sauvage: Violence, dépense et sacré dans l'art des années 1950–1960* (Paris, 2004)

Bois, Yve-Alain, 'Klein's Relevance for Today', *October*, 119 (Spring 2007)

Bonet, André, *Yves Klein, le peintre de l'infini* (Monaco, 2006)

Buchloh, Benjamin H. D., 'Klein and Poses', *Artforum International*, XXXIII/10 (Summer 1995)

——, 'Plenty or Nothing: From Yves Klein's Le Vide to Arman's Le Plein', in *Premises*: *Invested Spaces in Visual Arts, Architecture and Design from France, 1958–1998*, exh. cat., Guggenheim Museum Soho, New York (1998)

——, 'The Primary Colors for the Second Time: A Paradigm Repetition of the Neo-avant-garde', *October*, 37 (Summer 1986)

Cabañas, Kaira M., *The Myth of Nouveau Réalisme: Art and the Performative in Postwar France* (New Haven, CT, 2012)

——, 'Yves Klein's Performative Realism', *Grey Room*, 31 (Spring 2008)

Carrick, Jill, *Nouveau Réalisme, 1960s France, and the Neo-avant-garde: Topographies of Chance and Return* (Farnham, Surrey, 2010)

Charlet, Nicolas, *Les Ecrits d'Yves Klein* (Paris, 2005)

——, *Yves Klein* (Paris, 2000)

Cheetham, Mark A., 'Matting the Monochrome: Malevich, Klein, and Now', *Art Journal*, LXIV/4 (Winter 2005)

Clert, Iris, *Iris-Time (L'Aventure)* (Paris, 1978)

Debray, Cécile, ed., *Nouveau Réalisme*, exh. cat., Galerie Nationale du Grand Palais, Paris (2007)

Duve, Thierry de, *Cousus de fil d'or: Beuys, Warhol, Klein, Duchamp* (Villeurbanne, 1990)

Génévrier-Tausti, Terhi, *L'Envol d'ves Klein, l'origine d'une légende* (Paris, 2006)

Kahn, Annette, *Yves Klein: le maître du bleu* (Paris, 2000)

Klein-Moquay, Rotraut, and Robert Pincus-Witten, *Yves Klein USA* (Paris, 2009)

Ledeur, Jean-Paul, *Catalogue raisonné des éditions et des sculptures* (Sint-Martens-Latem, Belgium, 2000)

McEvilley, Thomas, *Yves: The Provocateur* (New York, 2010)

Millet, Catherine, *Yves Klein* (Paris, 1983)

O'Neill, Rosemary, *Art and Visual Culture on the French Riviera, 1956–1971* (Burlington, VT, 2012)

Périer, Henry, *Pierre Restany, l'alchimiste de l'art* (Paris, 1998)

Restany, Pierre, *Avec le Nouveau Réalisme sur l'autre face de l'art* (Nîmes, 2000)

——, *Yves Klein, le feu au coeur du vide* (Paris, 1990)

Ribettes, Jean-Michel, *Yves Klein contre C. G. Jung* (Brussels, 2003)

Riout, Denys, *La Peinture monochrome, Histoire et archéologie d'un genre* (Nîmes, 2003)

——, *Yves Klein. L'Aventure monochrome* (Paris, 2006)

——, *Yves Klein. Manifester l'immatériel* (Paris, 2004)

Robinson, Julia, ed., *New Realisms: 1957–1962: Object Strategies Between Readymade and Spectacle*, exh. cat., Museo Nacional Centro de Arte Reina Sofia, Madrid (2010)

Rosenthal, Nan, 'The Blue World of Yves Klein', PhD diss., Harvard University, 1976

Ruhnau, Werner, *Baukunst*: *Das Gelsenkirchener Theater. Yves Klein, Robert Adams, Paul Dierkes, Norbert Kricke, Jean Tinguely* (Dusseldorf, 1992)

Semin, Didier, *Le Peintre et son modèle déposé* (Geneva, 2001)

Yves Klein, exh. cat., Schirn Kunsthalle, Frankfurt (2004)

Yves Klein, exh. cat., ed. Sidra Stich (Ostfildern, 1994)

Yves Klein, exh. cat., Centre Georges Pompidou, Paris (1983)

Yves Klein, 1928–1962, A Retrospective, exh. cat., Institute for the Arts, Rice University, Houston (New York, 1982)

Yves Klein: Air Architecture, exh. cat., MAK Center for Art and Architecture, Los Angeles (2004)

Yves Klein /Claude Parent, Le Mémorial, Projet d'architecture, exh. cat., l'Espace de l'Art Concret, Mouans-Sartoux (2013)

Yves Klein: Corps, couleur, immatériel, exh. cat., Centre Georges Pompidou, Paris (2006)

Acknowledgements

A biography of Yves Klein is a collective endeavour and I wish to thank the community of scholars who have shared ideas and materials with me over the years, among them, Nan Rosenthal, Sidra Stich, John Rajchman, Denys Riout, Olivier Berggruen, Benjamin Buchloh, Kaira M. Cabañas, Laurence Bertrand-Dorléac, Yve-Alain Bois, Klaus Ottmann, Hannah Feldman, Natalie Adamson, Jonathan Crary, Tom McDonough, Branden Joseph, Francesco Pellizzi and Filippo Fimiani.

At Reaktion Books, I am grateful to Vivian Constantinoupoulos, who commissioned this book and whose patience and encouragement played an instrumental role at every stage of the process.

Finally I wish to thank my family and especially my lifelong inspiration, my grandmother, to whom this book is dedicated.